WILD AT HEART

DISCOVERING THE SECRET OF A MAN'S SOUL

UPDATED EDITION

STUDY GUIDE | SIX SESSIONS

JOHN ELDREDGE

WITH ALLEN ARNOLD

NELSON
BOOKS

An Imprint of Thomas Nelson

Published in Nashville, Tennessee, by Nelson Books. Nelson Books is a registered trademark of HarperCollins Christian Publishing, Inc.

Published in association with Yates & Yates, LLP, www.yates2.com.

All Scripture quotations, unless otherwise noted, are taken from the Holy Bible, New International Version®. NIV ®. Copyright 1973, 1978, 1984, 2011 by Biblica, Inc.®. Used by permission. All rights reserved worldwide.

Scripture quotations marked NIV 84 are taken from the Holy Bible, New International Version®. NIV ®. Copyright 1973, 1978, 1984, by Biblica, Inc.®. Used by permission. All rights reserved worldwide.

Scripture quotations marked NKJV taken from the New King James Version®. Copyright © 1982 by Thomas Nelson. Used by permission. All rights reserved.

Scripture quotations marked MSG are taken from THE MESSAGE, copyright © 1993, 2002, 2018 by Eugene H. Peterson. Used by permission of NavPress. All rights reserved. Represented by Tyndale House Publishers, Inc.

Scripture quotations marked NLT are taken from the Holy Bible, New Living Translation. © 1996, 2004, 2007, 2013, 2015 by Tyndale House Foundation. Used by permission of Tyndale House Publishers, Inc., Carol Stream, Illinois 60188. All rights reserved.

Thomas Nelson titles may be purchased in bulk for educational, business, fundraising, or sales promotional use. For information, please e-mail SpecialMarkets@ThomasNelson.com.

ISBN 978-0-310-12910-3 (softcover)
ISBN 978-0-310-12911-0 (ebook)

First Printing February 2020

CONTENTS

CONTENTS

INTRODUCTION

The way a man's life unfolds nowadays tends to drive his heart into remote regions of the soul. Endless hours at a computer screen; selling shoes at the mall; meetings, relentless texts, phone calls. The business world—where the majority of American men live and die—requires a man to be efficient and punctual. Corporate policies and procedures are designed with one aim: to harness a man to the plow and make him produce. But the soul refuses to be harnessed; it longs for passion, for freedom, for *life*. As D. H. Lawrence said, "I am not a mechanism."[1] A man needs to feel the rhythms of the earth; he needs to have in hand something real—the tiller of a boat, a set of reins, the roughness of rope, or simply a shovel. Can a man live all his days to keep his fingernails clean and trim? Is that what a boy dreams of?

Society at large can't make up its mind about men. Having spent the last thirty years redefining masculinity into something more sensitive, safe, manageable, and, well, feminine, it now berates men for not being men. Boys will be boys, they sigh. As though if a man were to truly grow up he would forsake wilderness and wanderlust and settle down, be at home forever in Aunt Polly's parlor. "Where are all the *real* men?" is regular fare for talk shows and new books. "You asked them to be women," I want to say. The result is a gender confusion never experienced at such a wide level in the history of the world.

How can a man know he is one when his highest aim is minding his manners?

Walk into most churches in America, have a look around, and ask yourself this question: What is a Christian man? Don't listen to what is said; look at what you find there. There is no doubt about it. You'd have to admit a Christian man is ... bored. At a recent church retreat I was talking with a guy in his fifties, listening really, about his own journey as a man. "I've pretty much tried for the last twenty years to be a good man as the church defines it." Intrigued, I asked him to say what he thought that was. He paused for a long moment. "Dutiful," he said. "And separated from his heart." *A perfect description*, I thought. *Sadly right on the mark.*

As Robert Bly lamented in *Iron John*, "Some women want a passive man if they want a man at all; the church wants a tamed man—they are called priests; the university wants a domesticated man—they are called tenure-track people; the corporation wants a ... sanitized, hairless, shallow man."[2] It all comes together as a sort of westward expansion against the masculine soul. And thus the *heart* of a man is driven into the high country, into remote places, like a wounded animal looking for cover. Women know this, and lament that they have no access to their man's heart. Men know it, too, but are often unable to explain why their heart is missing. They know their heart is on the run, but they often do not know where to pick up the trail. The church wags its head and wonders why it can't get more men to sign up for its programs. The answer is simply this: we have not invited a man to know and live from his deep heart.

But God made the masculine heart, set it within every man, and thereby offers him an *invitation*: come, and live out what I meant you to be. God *meant* something when he meant man, and if we are to ever find ourselves we must find that. What has he set in the masculine heart? Instead of asking what you think you ought to do to become a better man, I want to ask, *What makes you come alive?* What stirs your heart?

There are three desires I find written so deeply into my heart I know now I can no longer disregard them without losing my soul. They are core to who and what I am and yearn to be. I gaze into boyhood, I search the pages of Scripture and literature, I listen carefully to many, many men, and I am convinced these desires are universal, a clue into masculinity itself. They may be misplaced, forgotten, or misdirected, but in the heart of every man is a desperate desire for a battle to fight, an adventure to live, and a beauty to love.

This study guide is a companion to my book *Wild at Heart*. You can do this series as part of a group or on your own. Either way, you'll want to have a copy of the book and video series. You will note the book has twelve chapters, and this is a six-session study guide. Several sessions combine two chapters; others focus on one. Some chapters of the book are not included due to space. That's why we highly recommend reading the book in full in addition to being part of this study.

If you're leading a group, a guide has been provided for you in the back of this study. Each session in this guide follows this format:

- Welcome
- Video Summary
- Group Discussion
- Respond
- Closing Prayer
- Between-Sessions Personal Study (Five Days)
- Recommended Reading for Next Session

May God find you through these pages and restore you as his man.

John

THE HEART OF A MAN

A man's heart reflects the man . . .
PROVERBS 27:19 NIV 84

WELCOME

Welcome to session 1 of *Wild at Heart*. This first session covers chapter 1, "Wild at Heart," and chapter 2, "The Wild One Whose Image We Bear," of John's book. If there are new members in your group, take a moment to introduce yourselves to one another before watching the video. We suggest you simply share your name, some brief details about your life, and why you decided to join this study. Now, let's get started!

VIDEO TEACHING

Play the video segment for session 1. A summary of the key points is provided for your benefit as well as space to take additional notes.

Summary

In this six-part series, we are going to take a journey together into the most important part of your life—your masculine heart.

What does it mean to be a man? Is masculinity something that is just socially created?

Genesis 1:26-27 gives us insight into what God had in mind: "Then God said, 'Let us make mankind in our image, in our likeness, so that they may rule over the fish in the sea and the birds in the sky, over the livestock and all the wild animals, and over all the creatures that move along the ground.' So God created mankind in his own image, in the image of God he created them; male and female he created them."

Male and female he created us.

This is an absolutely incredible passage, because right here at the beginning, the very first things God says about the human race—about *you*—is that you are made in his image and that you are made in his image *as a man.*

Gender is from God. Masculinity is deep and immortal and everlasting.

God made the masculine heart and sets it within every man he creates. This is going to help us understand so much about our lives as men. If we know who we are, if we know what we were designed for, it will help us make sense of our stories and plan for our future.

Out of your masculine heart flows all of the things that make your life worth living—friendship, love, adventure, career, your dreams, and your relationship with God. If you look at the games that little boys play and the movies men love, you will find in every man's heart three core desires: a battle to fight, an adventure to live, and a beauty to love.

You simply have to get your heart back. This is like a treasure hunt with Indiana Jones. Only we're not looking for a golden statue; we're looking for something a whole lot more valuable than that.

Notes

GROUP DISCUSSION

Take a few minutes to go through the following questions with your group.

1. Could you relate to the stories and struggles of the men in this group? Why or why not?

2. What adventures or games did you play as a boy?

3. What is your favorite movie? Why are you drawn to it?

4. The core desires of a man's soul is a battle to fight, an adventure to live, and a beauty to love. How do you see these three desires expressing themselves in your life?

5. The Creator made the human race as male and female. Gender is from God. How would you describe what this truth means to you?

6. Where do you find yourself losing heart? Has greater duty or obligation helped in your attempts to awaken your heart? Explain.

RESPOND

Briefly review the summary for the session 1 teaching and any notes you took. In the space below, write down the most significant point you took away from this session.

CLOSING PRAYER

Wrap up your time together with prayer. Remember, prayer is simply talking to God. Here are a few ideas of what you could pray about based on the topics of this first session:

- Ask God to reveal why you're drawn to the movies you most love ... and what that reveals about your deepest longings.
- Invite God to reveal your true hunger for adventure, battle, and beauty.
- Confess how it is a hard time to be a man in the world today.
- Name the ways you've lost heart and your longing to get back what's been stolen.
- Speak Proverbs 4:23 aloud, asking God for help in guarding your heart.
- Pray that through this study, God would reveal more of your masculine heart.

SESSION 1

BETWEEN-SESSIONS PERSONAL STUDY

I n this section, you are invited to further explore the material in *Wild at Heart*. If you haven't already done so, read chapter 1, "Wild at Heart," and chapter 2, "The Wild One Whose Image We Bear," in the *Wild at Heart* book at this time. Each day's study in this section offers a short reading from John's book along with reflection questions designed to take you deeper into the themes of the study. Journal or just jot a few thoughts after each question. At the start of the next session, there will be a few minutes to share any insights . . . but remember that the primary goal of these questions is for your own personal growth and private reflection.

DAY ONE: A BATTLE TO FIGHT

There's a photo on my wall of a little boy about five years old, with a crew cut, big cheeks, and an impish grin. It's an old photograph, and the color is fading, but the image is timeless. It's Christmas morning 1964, and I've just opened what may have been the best present any boy received on any Christmas ever—a set of two pearl-handled six-shooters, complete with black leather holsters, a red cowboy shirt with two wild mustangs embroidered on either breast, shiny black boots, red bandanna, and straw hat. I've donned the outfit and won't take it off for weeks because, you see, this is not a "costume" at all; it's an *identity*.

Capes and swords, camouflage, bandannas and six-shooters, all the superhero outfits—these are the *uniforms* of boyhood. Little boys want to know they are powerful, they are dangerous, they are someone to be reckoned with. Despite what many modern educators would say, this is not a psychological disturbance brought on by violent television or chemical imbalance. Healthy aggression is part of the masculine *design*; we are hardwired for it. If we believe that man is made in the image of God, then we would do well to remember that "the LORD is a warrior; the LORD is his name" (Exodus 15:3). God is a warrior; man is a warrior.

Little girls do not invent games where large numbers of people die, where bloodshed is a prerequisite for having fun. Hockey, for example, was not a feminine creation. Nor was boxing. A boy wants to attack something—and so does a man, even if it's only a little white ball on a tee. He wants to whack it into kingdom come.

On the other hand, when my boys were growing up, they did not sit down to tea parties. They did not call their friends on the phone to talk about relationships. They grew bored of games that had no element of danger or competition or bloodshed. Cooperative games based on "relational interdependence" were complete nonsense. "No one is killed?" they asked, incredulous. "No one wins? What's the point?" Look at the global popularity of the video games boys and men play; they are overwhelmingly games of battle. The universal nature of this ought to have convinced us by now: The boy is a warrior; the boy is his name. And those are not boyish antics he is doing. When boys play at war, they are rehearsing their part in a much bigger drama. One day, you just might need that boy to defend you.

Those Union soldiers who charged the stone walls at Bloody Angle, or those Allied troops who hit the beaches at Normandy or the sands of Iwo Jima—what would they have done without this deep part of their heart? Life *needs* a man to be fierce—and fiercely devoted. The wounds he will take throughout his life will cause him to lose heart if all he has been trained to be is soft. This is especially true in the murky waters of relationships, where a man feels least prepared to advance. As Bly said, "In every relationship something *fierce* is needed once in a while."[4]

Now, this longing may have submerged from years of neglect, and a man may not feel that he is up to the battles he knows await him. Or it may have taken a very dark turn, as it has with inner-city gangs and terrorists. We need to heal the warrior heart in men, to be sure; set it in the service of goodness. Because the desire is there. Every man wants to play the hero. Every man *needs* to know that he is powerful. Women didn't make *Braveheart* one of the most popular films of its decade. *Saving Private Ryan, Top Gun,* the *Die Hard* films, *Gladiator,* the Star Wars and Marvel series, all the superhero blockbusters—the movies a man loves reveal what his heart longs for, what is set inside him from the day of his birth.

Like it or not, there is something fierce in the heart of every man. *Every* man.

John notes that as a boy, capes and swords, camouflage, bandannas and six-shooters, and all the superhero outfits weren't *costumes* but an *identity* to you. How did you find this to be true in your early life?

Life *needs* a man to be fierce—and fiercely devoted. What battle are you fiercely devoted to—and why?

"The LORD is a warrior; the LORD is his name" (Exodus 15:3). God is a warrior, and as men, we are created to be warriors. Is your "warrior heart" currently set in the service of goodness or playing out in destructive ways? Explain.

DAY TWO: AN ADVENTURE TO LIVE

I am no great hunter. I didn't play college football. In fact, in college I weighed 135 pounds and wasn't much of an athlete. Despite my childhood dreams, I have never been a racecar driver or a fighter pilot. I have no interest in televised sports. (Okay, except March Madness and the World Cup.) I don't like cheap beer, and though I do have an old Landcruiser, its tires are not ridiculously large. I say this because I anticipate that many readers—good men and women—will be tempted to dismiss this as some sort of macho-man pep rally. Not at all. *Wild at Heart* is not about becoming a lumberjack and drinking motor oil. I am simply searching, as many men (and hopeful women) are, for an authentic masculinity.

When winter failed to provide an adequate snow base, my boys would bring their sleds in the house and ride them down the stairs. My wife found them once with a rope out their second-story bedroom window, preparing to rappel down the side of the house. The recipe for fun is pretty simple when you're raising boys: add to any activity an element of danger, stir in a little exploration, add a dash of destruction, and you've got yourself a winner. The way they ski is a perfect example. Get to the top of the highest run, point your skis straight downhill and go, the faster the better. And this doesn't end with age; the stakes simply get higher.

A judge in his sixties, a real southern gentleman with a pinstriped suit and an elegant manner of speech, pulled me aside once during a conference. Quietly, almost apologetically, he spoke of his love for sailing, for the open sea, and how he and a buddy eventually built their own boat. Then came a twinkle in his eye. "We were sailing off the coast of Bermuda a few years ago, when we were hit by a northeaster [a raging storm]. Really, it came up out of nowhere. Twenty-foot swells in a thirty-foot homemade boat. I thought we were all going to die." A pause for dramatic effect, and then he confessed, "It was the best time of my life."

Compare your experience watching the latest James Bond or Star Wars thriller with, say, going to Bible study. The guaranteed success of each new release makes it clear—adventure is written into the heart of a man. And it's not just about having "fun." Adventure *requires* something of us, puts us to the test. Though we may fear the test, at the same time we yearn to be tested, to discover that we have what it takes.

That's why we set off down the Snake River against all sound judgment, why a buddy and I pressed on through grizzly country to find good fishing, why I went off to Washington, DC, as a young man to see if I could make it in those shark-infested waters. If a man has lost this desire, says he doesn't want it, that's only because he doesn't know he has what it takes, believes that he will fail the test. And so he decides it's better not to try. For reasons I hope to make clear later, most men hate the unknown and want to settle down and build their own city, get on top of their life.

But you can't escape it—there is something wild in the heart of every man.

Adventure is written into the heart of every man. What types of adventure set your heart racing? Why?

Have you ever passed on an adventure, deciding it was better to not try than risk failing the test? Describe how that affected your heart.

Real adventure requires something of us. It puts us to the test. How has a recent adventure tested you—and what did it reveal about you?

DAY THREE: A BEAUTY TO LOVE

Romeo has his Juliet, King Arthur fights for Guinevere, Robin rescues Maid Marian, and I will never forget the first time I kissed my grade-school sweetheart. It was in the fall of my seventh-grade year. I met Debbie in drama class, and fell absolutely head over heels. It was classic puppy love: I'd wait for her after rehearsals were over, carry her books back to her locker. We passed notes in class, talked on the phone at night.

I had never paid girls much attention, really, until now. This desire awakens a bit later in a boy's journey to manhood, but when it does his universe turns on its head. Anyway, I longed to kiss her but just couldn't work up the courage—until the last night of the school play. The next day was summer vacation, she was going away, and I knew it was now or never. Backstage, in the dark, I slipped her a quick kiss and she returned a longer one. Do you remember the scene from the movie *E.T.*, where the boy flies across the moon on his bike? Though I rode my little Schwinn home that night, I'm certain I never touched the ground.

There is nothing so inspiring to a man as a beautiful woman. She'll make you want to charge the castle, slay the giant, leap across the parapets. Or maybe, hit a home run. One day during a Little League game, my son Samuel was so inspired. He liked baseball, but most boys starting out aren't sure they really have it in them to be a great player. Sam was our firstborn, and like so many firstborns he was cautious.

He always let a few pitches go by before he took a swing, and when he did, it was never a full swing; every one of his hits up till that point were in the infield. Anyway, just as Sam stepped up to bat this one afternoon, his friend from down the street, a cute little blonde girl, showed up along the first-base line. Standing up on tiptoe, she yelled out his name and waved to Sam. Pretending he didn't notice her, he broadened his stance, gripped the bat a little tighter, looked at the pitcher with something fierce in his eye. First one over the plate he knocked into center field.

A man wants to be the hero to the beauty.

Young men going off to war carry a photo of their sweetheart in their wallet. Men who fly combat missions will paint a beauty on the side of their aircraft; the crews of the WWII B-17 bomber gave those flying fortresses names like *Me and My Gal* or the *Memphis Belle*. What would Robin Hood or King Arthur be without the woman they love? Lonely men fighting lonely battles. Indiana Jones and James Bond just wouldn't be the same without a beauty at their side, and inevitably they must fight for her.

You see, it's not just that a man needs a battle to fight; he needs someone to fight *for*. Remember Nehemiah's words to the few brave souls defending a wall-less Jerusalem? "Don't be afraid . . . fight for your brothers, your sons and your daughters, your wives and your homes" (Nehemiah 4:14 NIV 84). The battle itself is never enough; a man yearns for romance. It's not enough to be a hero; it's that he is a hero *to someone* in particular, to the woman he loves. Adam was given the wind and the sea, the horse and the hawk, but as God himself said, things were just not right until there was Eve.

Yes, there is something passionate in the heart of every man.

There is nothing so inspiring to a man as a beautiful woman. She'll make you want to charge the castle, slay the giant, leap across the parapets. How has this been true in your life?

It's not just that a man needs a battle to fight; he needs someone to fight *for*. Who is that beauty in your life?

Think of an example of pursuing the beauty in your life. How did that experience go?

DAY FOUR: BY WAY OF THE HEART

Which would you rather be said of you: "Harry? Sure, I know him. He's a real sweet guy." Or, "Yes, I know about Harry. He's a dangerous man . . . in a really good way." Ladies, how about you? Which man would you rather have as your mate? (Some women, hurt by masculinity gone bad, might argue for the "safe" man . . . and then wonder why, years later, there is no passion in their marriage, why he is distant and cold.)

I rest my case.

What if? What if those deep desires in our hearts are telling us the truth, revealing to us the life we were *meant* to live? God gave us eyes so that we might see; he gave us ears that we might hear; he gave us wills that we might choose, and he gave us hearts that we might *live*. The way we handle the heart is everything. A man must *know* he is powerful; he must *know* he has what it takes. A woman must *know* she is beautiful; she must *know* she is worth fighting for.

"But you don't understand," said one woman to me. "I'm living with a hollow man." No, it's in there. His heart is there. It may have evaded you, like a wounded animal, always out of reach, one step beyond your catching. But it's there. "I don't know when I died," said another man. "But I feel like I'm just using up oxygen." I understand. Your heart may feel dead and gone, but it's there. Something wild and strong and valiant, just waiting to be released.

Which would you rather be said of you by others—"I know him; he's a real sweet guy," or, "Yes, I know about him; he's a dangerous man . . . in a really good way." Why?

Which description do you think is a more accurate reflection of who you are *currently*?

Even if your heart feels dead and gone, something wild and strong and valiant is there, just waiting to be released. How does that make you feel?

DAY FIVE: WHERE DO WE COME FROM?

Who is this One we allegedly come from, whose image every man bears? What is he like? In a man's search for his strength, telling him that he's made in the image of God may not sound like a whole lot of encouragement at first. To most men, God is either distant or he is weak—the very thing they'd report of their earthly fathers.

Be honest now—what is your image of Jesus *as a man?* "Isn't he sort of meek and mild?" a friend remarked. "I mean, the pictures I have of him show a gentle guy with children all around. Kind of like Mother Teresa." Yes, those are the pictures I've seen myself in many churches. In fact, those are the *only* pictures I've seen of Jesus. They leave me with the impression that he was the world's nicest guy. Mister Rogers with a beard. Telling me to be like him feels like telling me to go limp and passive. Be nice. Be swell. Be like Mother Teresa.

I'd much rather be told to be like William Wallace.

Wallace, if you'll recall, is the hero of the film *Braveheart*. He is the warrior poet who came as the liberator of Scotland in the early 1300s—a true historical figure beloved by Scots to this day.

Now—is Jesus more like Mother Teresa or William Wallace? The answer is, it depends. If you're a leper, an outcast, a pariah of society whom no one has *ever* touched because you are "unclean," if all you have ever longed for is just one kind word, then Christ is the incarnation of tender mercy. He reaches out and touches you. On the other hand, if you're a Pharisee, one of those self-appointed doctrine police . . . watch out. On more than one occasion Jesus "picks a fight" with those notorious hypocrites.

Take the story of the crippled woman in Luke 13. Here's the background: The Pharisees are like the Scottish nobles— they, too, load heavy burdens on the backs of God's people but do not lift a finger to help them. What is more, they are so bound to the Law that they insist it is a sin to heal someone on the Sabbath, for that would be doing "work." They have twisted God's intentions so badly they think that man was made for the Sabbath, rather than the Sabbath for man (see Mark 2:27). Christ has already had a number of skirmishes with them, some over this very issue, leaving those quislings "wild with rage" (Luke 6:11 NLT).

Does Jesus tiptoe around the issue next time, so as not to "rock the boat" (the preference of so many of our leaders today)? Does he drop the subject in order to "preserve church unity"? Nope. He walks right into it, he baits them, he picks a fight. Let's pick up the story there:

One Sabbath day as Jesus was teaching in a synagogue, he saw a woman who had been crippled by an evil spirit. She had been bent double for eighteen years and was unable to stand up straight. When Jesus saw her, he called her over and said, "Woman, you are healed of your sickness!" Then he touched her, and instantly she could stand straight. How she praised and thanked God! But the leader in charge of the synagogue was indignant that Jesus had healed her on the Sabbath day. "There are six days of the week for working," he said to the crowd. "Come on those days to be healed, not on the Sabbath."

— LUKE 13:10-14 NLT

Can you believe this guy? What a weasel. Talk about missing the point. Christ is furious:

But the Lord replied, "You hypocrite! You work on the Sabbath day! Don't you untie your ox or your donkey from their

*stalls on the Sabbath and lead them out for water? Wasn't it
necessary for me, even on the Sabbath day, to free this dear
woman from the bondage in which Satan has held her for
eighteen years?" This shamed his enemies. And all the people
rejoiced at the wonderful things he did.*

— LUKE 13:15-17 NLT

Christ draws the enemy out, exposes him for what he is,
and shames him in front of everyone. The Lord is a *gentleman?!* Not if you're in the service of his enemy. God has a
battle to fight, and the battle is for our freedom.

To most men, God is either distant or he is weak—the very
thing they would report of their earthly fathers. Be honest
now—what is your image of God? Do you know where that
image of him came from?

Is your image of Jesus as a man more similar to Mister Rogers
or William Wallace? Why?

What most stood out to you about Jesus and his willingness to heal people on the Sabbath? How does that change or deepen your perception of his personality?

RECOMMENDED READING

Before your group gathers for the next session, read chapter 3, "The Question That Haunts Every Man," in *Wild at Heart*. This chapter will be the focus of session 2. Use the space below to write any key points or questions you want to bring to the next group meeting.

THE POSER

*The real tragedy of life is what dies
inside a man while he lives.*

NORMAN COUSINS

WELCOME

Welcome to session 2 of *Wild at Heart*. This second session covers chapter 3, "The Question That Haunts Every Man," of John's book. If there are new members in your group, take a moment to introduce yourselves to one another before watching the video. We suggest you simply share your name, some brief details about your life, and why you decided to join this study. Now, let's get started!

VIDEO TEACHING

Play the video segment for session 2. A summary of the key points is provided for your benefit as well as space to take additional notes.

Summary

What you meet when you meet a man is usually his fig leaf.

The successful guy. The really smart guy. The Bible guy.

Men stay where they feel powerful—or at least can convince other people they are. And they run from anything that makes them feel weak.

How do you act around your mechanic? The guys at the gym? Your boss? Your doctor?

In the search for genuine strength, we've got to be honest about the ways we are faking it.

Every boy has two questions in life. Do I have what it takes? Am I powerful? Most men live their lives either haunted by the Question or crippled by the answers they've been given.

The Poser is a brilliant counterfeit constructed out of our wounds and our sin. Early on in life, we learn what the world wants from us, and what it doesn't like so much. So we try and become what we think the world wants, and we leave huge parts of our heart behind.

That is our legacy from Adam. The bottom line is we are all sons of Adam. Most men are faking it. Whether hiding or presenting an "over-the-top" masculinity. None of this is meant to bring in shame or self-hatred.

We need to be honest about the Poser we have constructed, name it, face it, and lay it down in our search for a deep and genuine strength.

The thing I love about Jesus is how true he is. That trueness can be ours.

Notes

GROUP DISCUSSION

Take a few minutes to go through the following questions with your group.

1. What resonated with you about Bart's story of posing to try and make life work? Why?

2. Early in life, we learn what the world wants from us—and what it doesn't like. Where did you receive recognition early on as a boy? How did that shape what you pursued . . . and left behind?

3. As a man, what do you tend to avoid because it makes you feel weak, incompetent, or vulnerable? When did you first decide you weren't going to risk in this area—and why?

4. How would the people in your life describe you as a man?

5. How would you describe yourself as a man?

6. How do you think God sees you as a man?

RESPOND

Briefly review the summary for the session 2 teaching and any notes you took. In the space below, write down the most significant point you took away from this session.

CLOSING PRAYER

Wrap up your time together with prayer. Remember, prayer is simply talking to God. Here are a few ideas of what you could pray about based on the topics of this second session:

- Ask God to reveal the ways you tend to pose.
- Confess how you, like Adam, often hide from God.
- Invite God to reveal what's behind your fear of exposure.
- Release the fig leaves you use to fake it.
- Pray that God would help you live in trueness.

BETWEEN-SESSIONS PERSONAL STUDY

I n this section, you are invited to further explore the material in *Wild at Heart*. Each day's study in this section offers a short reading from chapter 3, "The Question That Haunts Every Man," of John's book, along with reflection questions designed to take you deeper into the themes of the study. Journal or just jot a few thoughts after each question. At the start of the next session, there will be a few minutes to share any insights . . . but remember that the primary goal of these questions is for your own personal growth and private reflection.

DAY ONE: OUR FEAR

I spent ten years of my life in the theater, as an actor and director. They were, for the most part, joyful years. I was young and energetic and pretty good at what I did. My wife was part of the theater company I managed, and we had many close friends there. I tell you this so that you will understand what I am about to reveal. In spite of the fact that my memories of theater are nearly all happy ones, I keep having this recurring nightmare.

This is how it goes: I suddenly find myself in a theater—a large, Broadway-style playhouse, the kind every actor aspires to play. The house lights are low and the stage lights full, so from my position onstage I can barely make out the audience, but I sense it is a full house. Standing room only. So far, so good. Actors love playing to a full house. But I am not loving the moment at all. I am paralyzed with fear. A play is under way, and I've got a crucial part. But I have no idea what play it is. I don't know what part I'm supposed to be playing; I don't know my lines; I don't even know my cues.

This is every man's deepest fear: to be exposed, to be found out, to be discovered as an impostor, and not really a man. The dream has nothing to do with acting; that's just the context for my fear. You have yours. A man bears the image of God in his strength, not so much physically but soulfully. Regardless of whether he knows the biblical account, if there's one thing a man does know he knows he is made to *come through*. Yet he wonders . . . *Can I? Will I?* When the going gets rough, when it really matters, will he pull it off?

For years my soul lived in this turmoil. I'd often wake in the morning with an anxiousness that had no immediate source. My stomach was frequently tied in knots. One day my dear friend Brent asked, "What do you do now that you don't act anymore?" I realized at that moment that my whole life felt like a performance, like I am always "on." I felt in every situation that I must prove myself again. After I spoke or taught a class, I'd hang on what others would say, hoping they would say it went well. Each counseling session felt like a new test: *Can I come through, again? Was my last success all that I had?*

Every man's deepest fear is to be exposed, to be found out, to be discovered as an impostor. How does this fear express itself in your life?

God has made us, as men, to "come through." Do you feel you have what it takes to come through? Why or why not?

Do you feel you are powerful? On what are you basing your answer?

DAY TWO: TWO LISTS

Honestly—how do you see yourself as a man? Are words like *strong, passionate,* and *dangerous* words you would choose? Do you have the courage to ask those in your life what *they* think of you as a man? What words do you fear they would choose? I've talked to many men about the film *Braveheart,* and though every single one of them would love to be William

Wallace, the dangerous warrior-hero, most see themselves as Robert the Bruce, the weak, intimidated guy who keeps folding under pressure. I'd love to think of myself as Indiana Jones; I'm afraid I'm more like Commodus in *Gladiator*.

The comedian Garrison Keillor wrote a very funny essay on this in *The Book of Guys*. Realizing one day that he was not being honest about himself as a man, he sat down to make a list of his strengths and weaknesses:

Useful Things I Can Do:

Be nice.

Make a bed.

Dig a hole.

Write books.

Sing alto or bass.

Read a map.

Drive a car.

Useful Things I Can't Do:

Chop down big trees and cut them into lumber or firewood.

Handle a horse, train a dog, or tend a herd of animals.

Handle a boat without panicking the others.

Throw a fastball, curve, or slider.

Load, shoot, and clean a gun. Or bow and arrow. Or use either of them, or a spear, net, snare, boomerang, or blowgun, to obtain meat.

Defend myself with my bare hands.[5]

Keillor confessed: "Maybe it's an okay report card for a *person* but I don't know any persons ... for a guy, it's not good."

What are the top three to five things on your list of "Useful Things You Can Do"? What are the top three to five on your list of "Useful Things You Can't Do"?

How do your responses in each list seem to answer the questions of "am I really a man—have got what it takes . . . when it counts?"

Would you risk asking those closest to you what they think of you as a man? What words do you fear they would choose?

DAY THREE: WHAT IS A MAN FOR?

Why does God create Adam? What is a man for? If you know what something is designed to do, then you know its purpose in life. A retriever loves the water; a lion loves the hunt; a hawk loves to soar. It's what they're made for. Desire reveals design, and design reveals destiny. In the case of human beings, our design is also revealed by our desires. Let's take adventure.

Adam and all his sons after him are given an incredible mission: rule and subdue, be fruitful and multiply. "Here is the entire earth, Adam. Explore it, cultivate it, care for it—it is your kingdom." Whoa . . . talk about an invitation. This is permission to do a heck of a lot more than cross the street. It's a charter to find the equator; it's a commission to build Camelot. Only Eden is a garden at that point; everything else is wild, so far as we know. No river has been charted, no ocean crossed, no mountain climbed. No one's discovered the molecule or fuel injection or created Beethoven's Fifth. It's a blank page, waiting to be written. A clean canvas, waiting to be painted.

Most men think they are simply here on earth to kill time—and it's killing them. But the truth is precisely the opposite. The secret longing of your heart, whether it's to build a boat and sail it, to write a symphony and play it, to plant a field and care for it—those are the things you were made to do. That's what you're here for. Explore, build, conquer—you don't have to tell a boy to do those things for the simple reason that it *is his purpose*. But it's going to take risk, and danger, and there's the catch—are we willing to live with the level of risk God invites us to? Something inside us hesitates.

Let's take another desire—why does a man long for a battle to fight? Because when we enter the story in Genesis, we step into a world at war. The lines have already been drawn. Evil is waiting to make its next move. Somewhere back before Eden, in the mystery of eternity past, there was a coup, a rebellion, an assassination attempt. Lucifer, the prince of angels, the captain of the guard, rebelled against the Trinity. He tried to take the throne of heaven by force, assisted by a third of the angelic army, in whom he instilled his own malice. They failed, and were hurled from the presence of the Trinity. But they were not destroyed, and the battle is not over. God now has an enemy . . . and so do we. Man is not born into a sitcom or a soap opera; he is born into a world at war. This is not *America's Got Talent*; it's *Saving Private Ryan*. There will be many, many battles to fight on many different battlefields.

And finally, why does Adam long for a beauty to love? Because there is Eve. He is going to need her, and she is going to need him. In fact, Adam's first and greatest battle is just about to break out, as a battle for Eve.

What is a man for? In your own words, why do you think God created Adam?

Now make it personal. Why do you think God created *you*?

God invites us, as men, into a certain level of risk and danger. What does that stir in you . . . and why?

DAY FOUR: DESIGNED TO COME THROUGH

Before Eve is drawn from Adam's side and leaves that ache that never goes away until he is with her, God gives Adam some instructions on the care of creation, and his role in the unfolding story. It's pretty basic, and very generous. "You may freely eat any fruit in the garden except fruit from the tree of the knowledge of good and evil" (Genesis 2:16–17 NLT). Okay, most of us have heard about that. But notice what God *doesn't* tell Adam.

There is no warning or instruction over what is about to occur: the temptation of Eve. This is just staggering. Notably missing from the dialogue between Adam and God is something like this: "Adam, one more thing. A week from Tuesday, about four in the afternoon, you and Eve are going to be down in the orchard and something dangerous is going to happen. Adam, are you listening? The eternal destiny of the human race hangs on this moment. Now, here's what I want you to do . . ." He doesn't tell him. He doesn't even mention it, so far as we know. Good grief—*why not?!* Because God *believes* in Adam. This is what he's designed to do—to come through. Adam doesn't need play-by-play instructions because this is what Adam is created *for*. It's already there, everything he needs, in his design, in his heart.

Needless to say, the story doesn't go well.

Adam fails; he fails Eve, and the rest of humanity. Let me ask you a question: Where is Adam, while the serpent is tempting Eve? He's standing right there: "She also gave some to her husband, who was with her. Then he ate it, too" (Genesis 3:6 NLT). The Hebrew for "with her" means right there, elbow to elbow. Adam isn't away in another part of the forest; he has no alibi. He is standing right there, watching the whole thing unravel. What does he do? Nothing. Absolutely nothing. He says not a word, doesn't lift a finger.[6] He won't risk, he won't fight, and he won't rescue Eve.

Our first father—the first real man—gave in to paralysis. He denied his very nature and went passive. And every man after him, every son of Adam, carries in his heart now the same failure. Every man repeats the sin of Adam, every day. We won't risk, we won't fight, and we won't rescue Eve. We truly are a chip off the old block.

Why do you think God, as far as we know, didn't give Adam any warning or instruction about the temptation of Eve?

Write Genesis 3:6 in the space below. Did you realize that Adam was standing right there with Eve when the whole thing unraveled? How does this passivity impact your perception of Adam's failure?

How do you see Adam's passivity at play in the ways you fail to risk or fight for what you love?

DAY FIVE: POSERS

Adam knows now that he has blown it, that something has gone wrong within him, that he is no longer what he was meant to be. Adam doesn't just make a bad decision; he *gives away* something essential to his nature. He is marred now, his strength is fallen, and he knows it. Then what happens? Adam hides.

"I was afraid because I was naked; so I hid" (Genesis 3:10).

You don't need a course in psychology to understand men. Understand that verse, let its implications sink in, and the men around you will suddenly come into focus. We are hiding, every last one of us. Well aware that we, too, are not what we were meant to be, desperately afraid of exposure, terrified of being seen for what we are and *are not*, we have run off into the bushes. We hide in our office, at the gym, behind the newspaper, and mostly *behind our personality*. Most of what you encounter when you meet a man is a facade, an elaborate fig leaf, a brilliant disguise.

Driving back from dinner one night, a friend and I were just sort of shooting the breeze about life and marriage and work. As the conversation deepened, he began to admit some of the struggles he was having. Then he came out with this confession: "The truth is, John, I feel like I'm just bs-ing my way through life, and that someday soon I'll be exposed as an impostor." I was so surprised. This is a popular, successful guy who most people like the moment they meet him. He's bright, articulate, handsome, and athletic. He's married to a beautiful woman, has a great job, drives a new truck, and lives in a big house. There is nothing on the outside that says, "not really a man." But inside, it's another story. It always is.

Truth be told, most of us are faking our way through life. We pick only those battles we are sure to win, only those adventures we are sure to handle, only those beauties we are sure we can love well.

Let me ask the guys who don't know much about cars: How do you talk to your mechanic? I know a bit about fixing cars, but not much, and when I'm around my mechanic I feel like a wuss. So what do I do? I fake it; I pose. I assume a sort of casual, laid-back manner I imagine "the guys" use when hanging around the lunch truck, and I wait for him to speak. "Looks like it might be your fuel mixture," he says. "Yeah, I thought it might be that." "When was the last time you had your carb rebuilt?" "Oh, I dunno . . . it's probably been years." (I'm guessing he's talking about my carburetor, and I have no idea if it's ever been rebuilt.)

Or how about you fellas who work in the corporate world? How do you act in the boardroom, when the heat is on? What do you say when the boss is riding you hard? "Jones, what the devil is going on down there in your division? You guys are three weeks late on that project!!" Do you try to pass the buck? "Actually, sir, we got the plans over to McCormick's department to bid the job weeks ago." Do you feign ignorance? "Really? I had no idea. I'll get right on it." Maybe you just weasel your way out of it: "That job's a slam dunk, sir. We'll have it done this week."

How about sports? A few years ago I volunteered to coach for my son's baseball team. There was a mandatory meeting that all coaches needed to attend before the season, to pick up equipment and listen to a "briefing." Our recreation department brought in a retired professional pitcher, a local boy, to give us all a pep talk. The posing that went on was incredible. Here's a bunch of balding dads with beer bellies sort of swaggering around, talking about their own baseball days, throwing out comments about pro players like they knew them personally, and spitting (I kid you not). Their "attitude" (that's a tame word) was so thick I needed waders. It was the biggest bunch of posers I've ever met—outside of church. That same sort of thing goes on Sunday mornings, it's just a different set of rules.

Adam doesn't just make a bad decision; he *gives away* something essential to his nature. What exactly does he give away? Why does this cause him to hide?

Where are you currently hiding and most afraid of exposure?

In what situations do you feel the Poser is most visible in your life? What could happen if you chose instead to risk offering your true self in these moments?

RECOMMENDED READING

Before your group gathers for the next session, read chapter 4, "The Wound," and chapter 7, "Healing the Wound," in *Wild at Heart*. These chapters will be the focus of session 3. Use the space provided to write any key points or questions you want to bring to the next group meeting.

THE WOUND

*The deepest desire of our hearts is for union
with God. God created us for union with himself:
This is the original purpose of our lives.*

BRENNAN MANNING

WELCOME

Welcome to session 3 of *Wild at Heart*. This third session covers chapter 4, "The Wound," and chapter 7, "Healing the Wound," of John's book. Let's get started!

VIDEO TEACHING

Play the video segment for session 3. A summary of the key points is provided for your benefit as well as space to take additional notes.

Summary

In this session, we get to the deeper issues. The healing of your wounded heart.

Every boy, in his journey to become a man, takes an arrow in the center of his heart, in the place of his strength. We receive these from brothers, mothers, coaches, and girlfriends. But the deepest wounds almost always come from our fathers. Did you know your dad adored you? Did he tell you a thousand times you have what it takes?

We are wounded, and with that wound comes a message—a lie about us, and about the world, and often about God too. The wound and lie then lead to a vow—a resolution to never, ever, do again whatever it was that might have brought the wound. This shapes us into the men we are—and are not—today as it plays out in a variety of ways, from anger and perfectionism to hiding and addictions.

We tend to mishandle our woundedness by minimizing it, denying it, or embracing the wound as what is most true about us. Yet the mission of Jesus is all about restoration. When asked about why he came, he quoted from Isaiah 61:1: "The Spirit of the Sovereign LORD is on me, because the LORD has anointed me to proclaim good news to the poor. He has sent me to bind up the brokenhearted, to proclaim freedom for the captives."

The truest thing about you is never your wound. Jesus came to heal your brokenness and restore you as a son . . . and as a man.

Notes

GROUP DISCUSSION

Take a few minutes to go through the following questions with your group.

1. How did Pablo's story shed light on the ways that we, as men, can be wounded?

2. What things did you do together with your dad when you were a child?

3. What was your dad's message to you in response to your question, "Do I have what it takes?"

4. What did your dad teach you about yourself as a man?

5. Will you risk sharing your wound? (If tears come . . . that's okay. This is part of the healing journey. Remember, everything said in this group is to remain in confidence.)

6. Men typically mishandle their woundedness by minimizing it, denying it, or embracing the wound as the truest thing about them. Which of these three describes how you have addressed your wounds? How has this approach worked for you?

RESPOND

Briefly review the summary for the session 3 teaching and any notes you took. In the space below, write down the most significant point you took away from this session.

CLOSING PRAYER

Wrap up your time together with prayer. Remember, prayer is simply talking to God. Here are a few ideas of what you could pray about based on the topics of this third session:

- Request God's interpretation of your childhood wounds.
- Confess your pain from your wounds, as David did in Psalm 109.
- Ask God for help in forgiving your father and others who wounded you.
- Trust God that your wounds aren't the truest part about you.
- Pray Isaiah 61:1, inviting Jesus to heal your heart and set you free.

SESSION 3

BETWEEN-SESSIONS PERSONAL STUDY

In this section, you are invited to further explore the material in *Wild at Heart*. Each day's study in this section offers a short reading from chapter 4, "The Wound," or chapter 7, "Healing the Wound," of John's book, along with reflection questions designed to take you deeper into the themes of the study. Journal or just jot a few thoughts after each question. At the start of the next session, there will be a few minutes to share any insights . . . but remember that the primary goal of these questions is for your own personal growth and private reflection.

DAY ONE: WHERE DOES MASCULINITY COME FROM?

In order to understand how a man receives a wound, you must understand the central truth of a boy's journey to manhood: masculinity is *bestowed*. A boy learns who he is and what he's got from a man, or the company of men. He cannot learn it any other place. He cannot learn it from other boys, and he cannot learn it from the world of women. The plan from the beginning of time was that his father would lay the foundation for a young boy's heart, and pass on to him that essential knowledge and confidence in his strength. Dad would be the first man in his life, and forever the most important man. Above all, he would answer *the question* for his son and give him his name. Throughout the history of man given to us in Scripture, it is the father who gives the blessing and thereby "names" the son.

Adam receives his name from God, and also the power of naming. He names Eve, and I believe it is therefore safe to say he also names their sons. We know Abraham names Isaac, and though Isaac's sons Jacob and Esau are apparently named by their mother, they desperately crave the *blessing* that can only come from their father's hand. Jacob gets the blessing, and nearly a century later, leaning on his staff, he passes it on to his sons—he gives them a name and an identity. "You are a lion's cub, O Judah . . . Issachar is a rawboned donkey . . . Dan will be a serpent . . . Gad will be attacked by a band of raiders, but he will attack them at their heels . . . Joseph is a fruitful vine . . . his bow remained steady" (Genesis 49:9, 14, 17, 19, 22, 24 NIV 84).

The Baptist's father names him John, even though the rest of the family was going to name him after his father, Zechariah. Even Jesus needed to hear those words of affirmation from his Father. After he is baptized in the Jordan, before the brutal attack on his identity in the wilderness, his Father speaks: "You are my Son, whom I love; with you I am well pleased" (Luke 3:22). In other words, "Jesus, I am deeply proud of you; you have what it takes."

One father-naming story in particular intrigues me. It centers around Benjamin, the last son born to Jacob. Rachel gives birth to the boy, but she will die as a result. With her last breath she names him Ben-Oni, which means "son of my sorrow." But Jacob intervenes and names him Benjamin—"Son of my right hand" (see Genesis 35:18). This is the critical move, when a boy draws his identity no longer from the mother, but from the father. Notice that it took an active *intervention* by the man; it always does.

Boys learn who they are and what they've got from a man, or the company of men. They cannot learn it from other boys or from the world of women. What was this experience—or lack of it—like for you as a boy?

Throughout the history of man given to us in Scripture, it is the father who gives the blessing and thereby "names" the son. What words did your father use to name you as a son? How did that impact your heart?

In Luke 3:22, God speaks words of affirmation over Jesus. Have you ever heard words like those Jesus did from his Father—"I am deeply proud of you; you have what it takes"? If so, what does that memory stir in you?

DAY TWO: THE FATHER-WOUND

Dave remembers the day the wound came. His parents were having an argument in the kitchen, and his father was verbally abusing his mother. Dave took his mom's side, and his father exploded. "I don't remember all that was said, but I do remember his last words: 'You are such a mama's boy,' he yelled at me. Then he walked out."

Perhaps if Dave had a strong relationship with his dad most of the time, a wound like this might be lessened, healed later by words of love. But the blow came after years of distance between them. Dave's father was often gone from morning till night with his own business, and so they rarely spent time together. What is more, Dave felt a lingering disappointment from his dad. He wasn't a star athlete, which he knew his dad highly valued. He had a spiritual hunger and often attended church, which his dad did not value. And so those words fell like a final blow, a death sentence.

Leanne Payne said that when the father-son relationship is right, "the quiet tree of masculine strength within the father protects and nurtures the fragile stripling of masculinity within his son."[7] Dave's father took an ax and gave his hardest blow to his young tree. How I wish it were a rare case, but I am deeply sorry to say I've heard countless stories like it.

In the case of violent fathers, the boy's question is answered in a devastating way. "Do I have what it takes? Am I a man, Papa?" *No, you are a mama's boy, an idiot, a seagull.* Those are defining sentences that shape a man's life. The assault wounds are like a shotgun blast to the chest. This can get unspeakably evil when it involves physical, sexual, or verbal abuse carried on for years. Without some kind of help, many men never recover. One thing about the assault wounds—they are obvious. The passive wounds are not; they are pernicious, like a cancer. Because they are subtle, they often go unrecognized as wounds and therefore are actually more difficult to heal.

My father was in many ways a good man. He introduced me to the West and taught me to fish and to camp. I still remember the fried egg sandwiches he would make us for dinner. It was his father's ranch that I worked on each summer, and my dad and I saw a lot of the West together as we'd make the long drive from Southern California to Oregon, often with fishing detours through Idaho and Montana. But like so many men of his era, my father had never faced the issues of his own wounds, and he fell to drinking when his life began to take a downhill turn. I was about eleven or twelve at the time—a very critical age in the masculine journey, the age when the question really begins to surface. At the very moment when I was desperately wondering what it means to be a man, and did I have what it takes, my father checked out, went silent. He had a workshop out back, attached to the garage, and he would spend his hours out there alone, reading, doing crossword puzzles, and drinking. That is a major wound.

Never receiving any sort of blessing from your father is a wound. Never spending time with him, or getting precious little time, that is wounding as well. My friend Alex's father died when he was four years old. The sun in his universe set, never to rise again. How is a little boy to understand that? Every afternoon Alex would stand by the front window, waiting for his father to come home. This went on for almost a year. I've had many clients whose fathers simply left and never came back. Stuart's dad did that, just up and left, and his mother, a troubled woman, was unable to raise him. So he was sent to his aunt and uncle. Divorce or abandonment is a wound that lingers because the boy believes if he had done things better, Daddy would have stayed.

Some fathers give a wound merely by their silence; they are present, yet absent to their sons. The silence is deafening.

I remember as a boy wanting my father to die, and feeling immense guilt for having such a desire. I understand now that I wanted someone to validate the wound. My father was gone, but because he was physically still around, he was not gone. So I lived with a wound no one could see or understand. In the case of silent, passive, or absent fathers, the question goes unanswered. "Do I have what it takes? Am I a man, Daddy?" Their silence is the answer: "I don't know . . . I doubt it . . . you'll have to find out for yourself . . . probably not."

Think back to your boyhood. How did your father answer your question, "Do I have what it takes? Am I a man, Daddy?"

Were the wounds from your father more aggressive or passive?

How have you carried the message of this wound into adulthood?

DAY THREE: THE WOUND'S EFFECT

Every man carries a wound. I have never met a man without one.

No matter how good your life may have seemed to you, you live in a broken world full of broken people. Your mother and father, no matter how wonderful, couldn't have been perfect. She is a daughter of Eve, and he a son of Adam. So there is no crossing through this country without taking a wound. They may come from other sources—a brother, an uncle, a coach, or a stranger. But come they do. And every wound, whether it's assaultive or passive, delivers with it a *message*.

The message feels final and true, absolutely true, because it is delivered with such force. Our reaction to it shapes our personality in very significant ways. From that flows the false self. Most of the men you meet are living out a false self, a pose, which is directly related to their wounds.

The message delivered with my wound (my father disappearing into his own battles) was simply this: *You are on your own, John. There is no one in your corner, no one to show you the way, and above all, no one to tell you if you are or are not a man. The core question of your soul has no answer, and can never get one.* What does a boy do with that? First, I became an unruly teen. I got kicked out of school, had a police record. We often misunderstand that behavior as "adolescent rebellion," but those are cries for involvement, for engagement. Even after God's dramatic rescue of me at the age of nineteen, when I became a Christian, the wound remained. As my dear friend Brent said, "Becoming a Christian doesn't necessarily fix things. My arrows were still lodged deep and refused to allow some angry wounds inside to heal."

I mentioned earlier that for years I was a very driven man, a perfectionist, a hard-charger, and a fiercely independent man. The world rewards that kind of drivenness; most of the successful men reading this book are driven. But behind me was a string of casualties—people I had hurt, or dismissed—including my own father. There was the near casualty of my marriage and there was certainly the casualty of my own heart. For to live a driven life you have to literally shove your heart down, or drive it with whips. You can never admit need, never admit brokenness. This is the story of the creation of that false self. And if you had asked my wife during the first ten years of our marriage if we had a good relationship, she probably would have said yes. But if you had asked her if something was missing, if she sensed a fatal flaw, she would have immediately been able to tell you: he doesn't need me. That was my vow, you see. *I won't need anyone.* After all, the wound was deep and unhealed, and the message it brought seemed so final: I am on my own.

Another friend, Stan, is a successful attorney and a genuinely good guy. When he was about fifteen, his father committed suicide—stuck a gun in his mouth and pulled the trigger. His family tried to put it all behind them, sweep it under the rug. They never spoke of it again. The message delivered by that gruesome blow was something like this: *Your background is very dark; the masculine in your family cannot even be spoken of; anything wild is violent and evil.* The effect was another sort of vow: "I will never do anything even remotely dangerous or risky or wild. I will never be like my dad (how many men live with that vow?). I won't take one step in that direction. I will be the nicest guy you ever met." You know what? He is. Stan's the nicest guy you could meet—gentle, creative, caring, soft-spoken. And now he hates that about himself; he hates the thought that he's a pushover, that he won't take you on, can't say no, can't stand up for himself.

Those are the two basic options. Men either overcompensate for their wound and become driven (violent men), or they shrink back and go passive (retreating men). Often it's an odd mixture of both.

The wound comes, and with it a message. From that place the boy makes a vow, chooses a way of life that gives rise to the false self. At the core of it all is a deep uncertainty. The man doesn't live from a center. So many men feel stuck—either paralyzed and unable to move, or unable to stop moving.

What is the vow you've made in response to the message of your wounds?

Men either overcompensate for their wound and become determined to prove the message wrong, or they shrink back, attempting to avoid the "certainty" of the wound's message. Often it's a mixture of both. What has your experience been on this front?

What impact has this message had on your relationships, habits, and daily life as a man?

DAY FOUR: HEALING THE WOUND (PART 1)

There are no formulas with God. The way in which God heals our wound is a deeply personal process. He is a person and he insists on working personally. For some, it comes in a moment of divine touch. For others, it takes place over time and through the help of another, maybe several others. As Agnes

Sanford said, "There are in many of us wounds so deep that only the mediation of someone else to whom we may 'bare our grief' can heal us."[8]

So much healing took place in my life simply through my friendship with Brent. We were partners, but far more than that, we were friends. We spent hours together fly-fishing, backpacking, hanging out in pubs. Just spending time with a man I truly respected, a real man who loved and respected me—nothing heals quite like that.

At first I feared that I was fooling him, that he'd see through it any day and drop me. But he didn't, and what happened instead was validation. My heart knew that if a man I *know* is a man thinks I'm one, too, well then, maybe I am one after all. Remember—masculinity is bestowed by masculinity. But there have been other significant ways in which God has worked—times of healing prayer, times of grieving the wound and forgiving my father. Most of all, times of deep communion with God. The point is this: healing never happens outside of intimacy with Christ. The healing of our wound flows out of our union with him.

But there are some common themes that I share with you as you seek the restoration of your heart. In today's reading, we'll look at the first step.

Step one: Surrender. It seems so simple it's almost hard to believe we overlook it, never ask for it, and when we do, we sometimes struggle for days just to get the words out.

It begins with surrender. As C. S. Lewis said, "Until you have given yourself to him you will not have a real self."[9] We return the branch to its trunk; we yield our lives to the One who is our Life. And then *we invite Jesus into the wound*; we ask him to come and meet us there, to enter into the broken and

unhealed places of our heart. When the Bible tells us that
Christ came to redeem mankind, it offers a whole lot more
than forgiveness. To simply forgive a broken man is like telling someone running a marathon, "It's okay that you've
broken your leg. I won't hold that against you. Now finish the
race." That is cruel, to leave him disabled that way. No, there
is much more to our redemption. The core of Christ's mission
is foretold in Isaiah 61:

> *The Spirit of the Sovereign* LORD *is on me,*
> *because the* LORD *has anointed me*
> *to preach good news to the poor.*
> *He has sent me to bind up the brokenhearted,*
> *to proclaim freedom for the captives*
> *and release . . . for the prisoners* (verse 1 NIV 84)

The Messiah will come, he says, to bind up and heal, to
release and set free. To heal, release, and set free what? *Your
heart.* Christ comes to restore and release you, your soul, the
true you. This is *the* central passage in the entire Bible about
Jesus, the one he chooses to quote about himself when he
steps into the spotlight in Luke 4 and announces his arrival.
So take him at his word—ask him in to heal all the broken
places within you and unite them into one whole and healed
heart. Ask him to release you from all bondage and captivity,
as he promised to do. As George MacDonald prayed, "Gather
my broken fragments to a whole . . . Let mine be a merry, all-
receiving heart, but make it a whole, with light in every part."[10]

But you can't do this at a distance; you can't ask Christ
to come into your wound while you remain far from it. You
have to go there with him.

Lord Jesus, I give my life to you—everything I am, everything I have become. I surrender myself to you utterly. Come and be my Lord. Be my healer. I give you my wounded heart. Come and meet me here. Enter my heart and soul, my wounds and brokenness, and bring your healing love to me in these very places.

The way in which God heals our wound is a deeply personal process. He is a person, and he insists on working personally. Do you sometimes wish God would offer a generic formula for your healing—or do you see the beauty in how he personally comes after your heart? Explain.

You can't ask Christ to come into your wound while you remain far from it. How does this truth change the way you approach healing?

The healing process begins with our surrender. What is it that you find hardest to surrender to God as you enter into this process?

DAY FIVE: HEALING THE WOUND (PART 2)

The first step to healing our wound, covered in the last reading, is Surrender. Today, we will look at the remaining three steps.

Step two: We grieve. We must grieve the wound. It was not your fault, and it did matter. Oh what a milestone day that was for me when I simply allowed myself to say that the loss of my father *mattered*. The tears that flowed were the first I'd ever granted my wound, and they were deeply healing. All those years of sucking it up melted away in my grief.

It is so important for us to grieve our wound; it is the only honest thing to do. For in grieving we admit the truth—that we were hurt by someone we loved, that we lost something very dear, and it hurt us very much. Tears are healing. They help to open and cleanse the wound. As Augustine wrote in his *Confessions*, "The tears . . . streamed down, and I let them flow as freely as they would, making of them a pillow for my heart. On them it rested."[11] Grief is a form of validation; it says the wound *mattered*.

Step three: We let God love us. We let God love us; we let him get really close to us. I know, it seems painfully obvious, but I'm telling you few men are ever so vulnerable as to simply let themselves be loved by God. Abiding in the love of God is our only hope, the only true home for our hearts. It's not that we mentally acknowledge that God loves us. It's that we let our hearts come home to him, and stay in his love. MacDonald said it this way:

> When our hearts turn to him, that is opening the door to him . . . then he comes in, not by our thought only, not in our idea only, but he comes himself, and of his own will.

*Thus the Lord, the Spirit, becomes the soul of our souls . . .
Then indeed we are; then indeed we have life; the life of
Jesus has . . . become life in us . . . we are one with God for-
ever and ever.*[12]

Step four: We forgive. Time has come for us to forgive our
fathers and all those who have wounded us. Paul warns us
that unforgiveness and bitterness can wreck our lives and the
lives of others (see Ephesians 4:31; see also Hebrews 12:15).
As someone has said, forgiveness is setting a prisoner free and
then discovering the prisoner was you. I found some help in
Robert Bly's experience of forgiving his own father, when he
said, "I began to think of him not as someone who had
deprived me of love or attention or companionship, but as
someone who himself had been deprived, by his father and
his mother and by the culture."[13] My father had his own
wound that no one ever offered to heal. His father was an
alcoholic, too, for a time, and there were some hard years for
my dad as a young man just as there were for me.

Now, you must understand—forgiveness is a choice. It is
not a feeling, but an act of the will. As Neil Anderson has
written, "Don't wait to forgive until you feel like forgiving;
you will never get there. Feelings take time to heal after the
choice to forgive is made."[14] We allow God to bring the hurt
up from our past, for "if your forgiveness doesn't visit the
emotional core of your life, it will be incomplete."[15] We
acknowledge that it hurt, that it mattered, and we choose to
extend forgiveness to our father. This is *not* saying, "It didn't
really matter"; it is *not* saying, "I probably deserved part of
it anyway." Forgiveness says, "It was wrong, it mattered, and
I release you."

I hope you find these steps immensely helpful in healing your wound.

Only when you enter your wound will you discover your true glory. There are two reasons for this. First, because the wound was given in the place of your true strength, as an effort to take you out. Until you go there you are still posing, offering something more shallow and insubstantial. And therefore, second, it is out of your brokenness that you discover what you have to offer the community. The false self is never wholly false. Those gifts we've been using are often quite true about us, but we've used them to hide behind. We thought that the power of our life was in the golden bat, but the power is in *us*. When we begin to offer not merely our gifts but our true selves, that is when we become powerful.

Grief is a form of validation; it says the wound *mattered*. Have you ever grieved your wound? If not, why not?

Allowing God to love us means letting him get really close to us. Why do you think, as men, we struggle in this area?

Forgiving another person is not saying it didn't matter. Forgiveness says, "It was wrong, it mattered, and I release you." Who do you need to forgive now in order to gain further healing? Will you do so? Why or why not?

RECOMMENDED READING

Before your group gathers for the next session, read chapter 8, "A Battle to Fight: The Enemy," and chapter 9, "A Battle to Fight: The Strategy," in *Wild at Heart*. These chapters will be the focus of session 4. Use the space below to write any key points or questions that you want to bring to the next group meeting.

THE BATTLE

Enemy-occupied territory—
that is what this world is.

C.S. LEWIS

WELCOME

Welcome to session 4 of *Wild at Heart.* This fourth session covers chapter 8, "A Battle to Fight: The Enemy," and chapter 9, "A Battle to Fight: The Strategy," of John's book. Let's get started!

VIDEO TEACHING

Play the video segment for session 4. A summary of the key points is provided for your benefit as well as space to take additional notes.

Summary

In this session, we turn the corner to explore what it looks like to live from our deep masculine hearts in the realm of battle, adventure, and beauty.

God, who is a great warrior, created man in his image. God set within us a warrior heart because he has created us to join him in his war against evil. If we're going to find our part in God's story, if we're going to be the men that he made us to be, we have got to get that part of our heart back.

We want to be the hero . . . but something happens in the story of boy to man. The wounds come. The poser is created. On top of that, the world we live in emasculates men. What we are left with is a world of Really Nice Guys.

But let's go back to the movies we love. Regardless of the movie, the hero must engage in a battle of some kind. Why? Because they all have a villain—from Darth Vader and Sauron to Longshanks and Commodus.

Why does every story have a villain? Because ours does.

In Scripture, we are told: "Be alert and of sober mind. Your enemy the devil prowls around like a roaring lion looking for someone to devour. Resist him, standing firm in the faith, because you know that the family of believers throughout the world is undergoing the same kind of sufferings" (1 Peter 5:8–9).

We have been born into a world at war. And we have a role to play in this unfolding story.

A man needs a battle to fight. He needs a place for the warrior in him to come alive and be honed, trained, seasoned. If we can reawaken that fierce quality in a man, hook it up to a higher purpose, and release the warrior within, then the boy can grow up and become truly masculine.

Every man is a warrior, yet every man must choose to fight. The warrior is not the only role a man must play; there are others we will explore in later sessions. But the warrior is crucial in our movement toward any masculine integrity. It is hardwired into every man.

The recovery of our warrior heart is absolutely essential.

Notes

GROUP DISCUSSION

Take a few minutes to go through the following questions with your group.

1. In Sam's battle, how did you see his warrior heart come out?

2. God set within every man a warrior heart. What is one way that you have seen this essential aspect of who you are impact your world for good?

3. What is an example of how your warrior heart responds in not so good ways?

4. We could probably divide all guys into three categories: (1) guys who have no battle, (2) guys who are fighting the wrong battles, and (2) guys who know their true place in the battle. Which category do you see yourself in now? Explain.

5. What is the biggest battle you're fighting now in your life?

6. Until now, have you considered spiritual warfare a major category for the battles that have come against you? Why or why not?

RESPOND

Briefly review the summary for the session 4 teaching and any notes you took. In the space below, write down the most significant point you took away from this session.

CLOSING PRAYER

Wrap up your time together with prayer. Remember, prayer is simply talking to God. Here are a few ideas of what you could pray about based on the topics of this fourth session:

- Ask God to reveal his role as a warrior (see Exodus 15:3).
- Pray for God to awaken the warrior heart he has set within you.
- Express your desire for the right battles to fight.
- Request that God keep you away from the wrong battles.
- Ask God for eyes to see the spiritual warfare coming against you.
- Ask for strength to resist the devil so that he will flee (see 1 Peter 5:8–9).

BETWEEN-SESSIONS
PERSONAL STUDY

I n this section, you are invited to further explore the material in *Wild at Heart*. Each day's study in this section offers a short reading from chapter 8, "A Battle to Fight: The Enemy," or chapter 9, "A Battle to Fight: The Strategy," of John's book, along with reflection questions designed to take you deeper into the themes of the study. Journal or just jot a few thoughts after each question. At the start of the next session, there will be a few minutes to share any insights . . . but remember that the primary goal of these questions is for your own personal growth and private reflection.

DAY ONE: THE WARRIOR HEART

A man must have a battle to fight, a great mission to his life that involves and yet transcends even home and family. He must have a cause to which he is devoted even unto death, for this is written into the fabric of his being. Listen carefully now: *you do*. That is why God created you—to be his intimate *ally*, to join him in the Great Battle. You have a specific place in the line, a mission God made you for. Winston Churchill was called upon to lead the British through the desperate hours of World War II. He said, "I felt as if I were walking with destiny, and that all my past life had been but a preparation for this hour and for this trial."[16] The same is true of you; your whole life has been preparation.

"I'd love to be William Wallace, leading the charge with a big sword in my hand," sighed a friend. "But I feel like I'm the guy back there in the fourth row, with a hoe." That's a lie of the Enemy—that your place is really insignificant, that you aren't really armed for it anyway. In your life you *are* William Wallace—who else could be? There is no other man who can replace you in your life, in the arena you've been called to. If you leave your place in the line, it will remain empty. No one else can be who you are meant to be. You *are* the hero in your story. Not a bit player, not an extra, but the main man. This is the next leg in the initiation journey, when God calls a man forward to the front lines. He wants to develop and release in us the qualities every warrior needs—including a keen awareness of the enemies we will face.

Above all else, a warrior has a *vision*; he has a transcendence to his life, a cause greater than self-preservation. The root of all our woes and our false self was this: we were seeking to save our life and we lost it. Christ calls a man beyond that; "whoever loses his life for me and for the gospel will save it" (Mark 8:35 NIV 84). Again, this isn't just about being willing to die for Christ; it's much more daily than that. For years all my daily energy was spent trying to beat the trials in my life and arrange for a little pleasure. My weeks were wasted away either striving or indulging. I was a mercenary.

A mercenary fights for pay, for his own benefit; his life is devoted to himself. A true warrior serves something—or Someone—higher than himself.

As men, we must have a battle to fight. What is the great mission of your life? What are the stakes?

You are God's intimate ally in the Great Battle. What does that stir in your heart?

There is no other man who can replace you in your life, in the arena to which you've been called. If you leave your place in the line, it will remain empty. No one else can be who you are meant to be. Given that, who exactly are you meant to be?

DAY TWO: THE TRAITOR WITHIN

A warrior is *cunning*. He knows when to fight and when to run; he can sense a trap and never charges blindly ahead; he knows what weapons to carry and how to use them. Whatever specific terrain you are called to—at home, at work, in the realm of the arts or industry or world politics—you will always encounter three enemies: the world, the flesh, and the devil. They make up a sort of unholy trinity. Because they always conspire together it's a bit difficult to talk about them individually; in any battle at least two of them are involved, but usually it's all three. Still, they each have their own personality, so I'll take them one at a time and then try to show how they collude against us. Let's start with the enemy closest at hand.

John Owen writes, "However strong a castle may be, if a treacherous party resides inside (ready to betray at the first opportunity possible), the castle cannot be kept safe from the enemy. There are traitors in our hearts, ready to take part, to close and side with every temptation, and to give up all to them."[17] Ever since that fateful day when Adam gave away the essence of his strength, men have struggled with a part of themselves that is ready at the drop of a hat to do the same. We don't want to speak up unless we know it will go well, and we don't want to move unless we're guaranteed success.

What the Scriptures call the flesh, the old man, or the sinful nature, is that part of fallen Adam in every man that always wants the easiest way out. It's much easier to masturbate than to make love to your wife, especially if things are not well between you and initiating sex with her feels risky. It's much easier to go down to the driving range and attack a bucket of balls than it is to face the people at work who are angry at you. It's much easier to clean the garage, organize your files, cut the grass, or work on the car than it is to talk to your teenage daughter.

To put it bluntly, your flesh is a weasel, a poser, and a selfish pig. And your flesh is *not you*. Did you know that? Your flesh is not the real you. When Paul gives us his famous passage in Romans 7 on what it's like to struggle with sin, he tells a story we are all too familiar with:

> *I decide to do good, but I don't really do it; I decide not to do bad, but then I do it anyway. My decisions, such as they are, don't result in actions. Something has gone wrong deep within me and gets the better of me every time. It happens so regularly that it's predictable. The moment I decide to do good, sin is there to trip me up. I truly delight in God's commands, but it's pretty obvious that not all of me joins in that delight. Parts of me covertly rebel, and just when I least expect it, they take charge.*
>
> ROMANS 7:17–25 MSG

Okay, we've all been there many times. But what Paul concludes is just astounding: "I am not really the one doing it; the sin within me is doing it" (Romans 7:20 NLT). Did you notice the distinction he makes? Paul says, "Hey, I know I struggle with sin. But I also know that *my sin is not me*—this is not my true heart." You are not your sin; sin is no longer the truest thing about the man who has come into union with Jesus. Your heart is good. "I will give you a new heart and put a new spirit in you" (Ezekiel 36:26).

The Big Lie in the church today is that you are nothing more than "a sinner saved by grace." You are a lot more than that. You are a new creation in Christ. The New Testament calls you a saint, a holy one, a son of God. In the core of your being you are a good man. Yes, there is a war within us, but it is a *civil* war. The battle is not between us and God.

The *real* you is on the side of God against the false self. Knowing this makes all the difference in the world.

Who are the three enemies that you will always encounter?

What is a recent example of how the traitor within tried to sabotage the real you?

Your sin is not you. The battle is not between you and God . . . but between you and your false self. How does that change your perception of the sins with which you struggle?

DAY THREE: THE WORLD

What is this enemy that the Scripture calls "the world"? Is it drinking and dancing and smoking? Is it going to the movies or playing cards? That is a shallow and ridiculous approach to holiness. It numbs us to the fact that good and evil are much more serious. The Scriptures never prohibit drinking alcohol, only drunkenness; dancing was a vital part of King David's life; and while there are some very godly movies out there, there are also some very ungodly churches. No, "the world" is not a place or a set of behaviors—it is any system built by our collective sin, all our false selves coming together to reward and destroy each other. Take all those posers out there, put them together in an office or a club or a church, and what you get is what the Scriptures mean by "the world."

The world is a carnival of counterfeits—counterfeit battles, counterfeit adventures, counterfeit beauties. Men should think of it as a corruption of their strength. Battle your way to the top, says the world, and you are a man. Why is it then that the men who get there are often the emptiest, most frightened, prideful posers around? They are mercenaries, battling only to build their own kingdoms. There is nothing transcendent about their lives. The same holds true of the adventure addicts; no matter how much you spend, no matter how far you take your hobby, it's still merely that—a hobby. And as for the counterfeit beauties, the world is constantly trying to tell us that the Woman with Golden Hair is out there—go for her.

The world offers a man a false sense of power and a false sense of security. Be brutally honest now—where does your own sense of power come from? Is it how pretty your wife is—or your secretary? Is it how many people attend your church? Is it *knowledge*—that you have an expertise and that makes others come to you, bow to you? Is it your position, degree, or title? A white coat, a PhD, a podium, or a paneled office can make a man feel like pretty neat stuff. What happens inside you when I suggest you give it up?

Put the book down for a few moments and consider what you would think of yourself if tomorrow you lost everything that the world has rewarded you for. "In whatever man does without God," said George MacDonald, "he must fail miserably—or succeed more miserably."[18] Jesus warns us against anything that gives a false sense of power. When you walk into a company dinner or a church function, he said, take a back seat. Choose the path of humility; don't be a self-promoter, a glad-hander, a poser. Climb *down* the ladder; have the mail clerk over for dinner; treat your secretary like she's more important than you; look to be the servant of all. *Where am I deriving my sense of strength and power from?* is a good question to ask yourself . . . often.

If you want to know how the world *really* feels about you, just start living out of your true strength. Say what you think, stand up for the underdog, challenge foolish policies. They'll turn on you like sharks.

The world of posers is shaken by a real man. They'll do whatever it takes to get you back in line—threaten you, bribe you, seduce you, undermine you. They crucified Jesus. But it didn't work, did it? You must let your strength show up. Remember Christ in the Garden, the sheer force of his presence? Many of us have actually been afraid to let our strength show up because the world doesn't have a place for it. Fine. The world's screwed up. Let people feel the weight of who you are and let them deal with it.

When Scripture talks about "the world," it is not a place or a set of behaviors—but rather any system built by our collective sin, all our false selves coming together to reward and destroy each other. How does this definition change how you see the world around you?

The world is a carnival of counterfeits—counterfeit battles, counterfeit adventures, counterfeit beauties. Which counterfeits tend to distract you the most? Why?

Many men are afraid to let their strength show up because the world doesn't have a place for it. How would things change if you let people feel the weight of who you are and deal with it?

DAY FOUR: THE DEVIL

The devil no doubt has a place in our theology, but is he a category we even think about in the daily events of our lives?

Has it ever crossed your mind that not every thought that crosses your mind comes from you? It happens all the time in marriages, in ministries, in any relationship. We are being lied to all the time. Yet we never stop to say, "Wait a minute... who else is speaking here? Where are those ideas coming from? Where are those *feelings* coming from?" If you read the saints from every age before the Modern Era—that pride-filled age of reason, science, and technology we all were thoroughly educated in—you'll find that they take the devil very seriously indeed. As Paul said, "We are not unaware of his schemes" (2 Corinthians 2:11). But we, the enlightened, have a much more commonsense approach to things. We look for a psychological or physical or even political explanation for every trouble we meet.

Who caused the Chaldeans to steal Job's herds and kill his servants? Satan, clearly (see Job 1:12, 17). Yet do we even give him a passing thought when we hear of terrorism today? Who kept that poor woman bent over for eighteen years, the one Jesus healed on the Sabbath? Satan, clearly (see Luke 13:16). But do we consider him when we are having a headache that keeps us from praying or reading Scripture? Who moved Ananias and Sapphira to lie to the apostles? Satan again (see Acts 5:3). But do we really see his hand behind a fallout or schism in ministry? Who was behind that brutal assault on your own strength, those wounds you've taken? As William Gurnall said, "It is this image of God reflected in you that so enrages hell; it is this at which the demons hurl their mightiest weapons."[19]

There is a whole lot more going on behind the scenes of our lives than most of us have been led to believe. Behind the world and the flesh is an even more deadly enemy . . . one we rarely speak of and are even much less ready to resist. Yet this is where we live now—on the front lines of a fierce spiritual war that is to blame for most of the casualties you see around you and most of the assault against you. It's time we prepared ourselves for it.

Paul makes this statement about Satan: "We are not unaware of his schemes" (2 Corinthians 2:11). Do his words describe your awareness? Or are you more likely to blame the enemy's schemes on natural or human causes? Explain.

On any given day, which world seems most real to you—the world of drive-thru coffee shops, carpools, and office politics; or the unseen kingdom of God, angels, and spiritual warfare? Why do you think this is the case?

Scripture tells us how to combat the enemy: "Submit your-selves, then, to God. Resist the devil, and he will flee from you" (James 4:7). Have you tried to resist the enemy in this way? If so, what has been the result?

DAY FIVE: THE WEAPONS OF WAR

Most men have a hard time sustaining any sort of devotional life because it has no vital connection to recovering and protecting their strength; it feels about as important as flossing. But if you saw your life as a great battle and you *knew* you needed time with God for your very survival, you would do it. Maybe not perfectly—nobody ever does, and that's not the point anyway—but you would have a reason to seek him. We give a half-hearted attempt at the spiritual disciplines when the only reason we have is that we "ought" to. But we'll find a way to make it work when we are convinced we're history if we don't.

That God has provided weapons of war for us sure makes a lot more sense if our days are like a scene from *Saving Private Ryan*. How many Christians have read over those passages about the shield of faith and the helmet of salvation and never really known what to do with them? *What lovely poetic imagery; I wonder what it means.* It means that God has given you armor and you'd better put it on. Every day. This equipment is really there, in the spiritual, unseen realm. We don't see it, but the angels and our enemies do. Start by simply praying through the passage in Ephesians as if suiting up for the arena:

> *"Therefore put on the full armor of God, so that when the day of evil comes, you may be able to stand your ground, and after you have done everything, to stand. Stand firm then, with the belt of truth buckled around your waist . . ."* Lord, I put on the belt of truth. I choose a lifestyle of honesty and integrity. Show me the truths I so desperately need today. Expose the lies I'm not even aware that I'm believing. *". . . with the breastplate of righteousness in place . . ."* And yes, Lord, I wear your righteousness today against all condemnation and corruption. Fit me with your holiness and purity—defend me from all assaults against my heart. *". . . and with your feet fitted with the readiness that comes from the gospel of peace . . ."* I do choose to live for the gospel at any moment. Show me where the larger story is unfolding and keep me from being so lax that I think the most important thing today is the soap operas of this world.
>
> *"In addition to all this, take up the shield of faith, with which you can extinguish all the flaming arrows of the evil one . . ."* Jesus, I lift against every lie and every assault the confidence that you are good, and that you have good in store for me. Nothing is coming today that can overcome me because you are with me. *". . . Take the helmet of salvation . . ."* Thank you, Lord, for my salvation. I receive it in a new and fresh way from you and I declare that nothing can separate me now from the love of Christ and the place I shall ever have in your kingdom. *". . . and the sword of the Spirit,*

which is the word of God . . ." Holy Spirit, show me specifically today the truths of the Word of God that I will need to counter the assaults and the snares of the Enemy. Bring them to mind throughout the day. ". . . And pray in the Spirit on all occasions with all kinds of prayers and requests. With this in mind, be alert and always keep on praying for all the Lord's people." Finally, Holy Spirit, I agree to walk in step with you in everything—in all prayer as my spirit communes with you throughout the day (6:13–18).

One more thing: don't even think about going into battle alone. Don't even try to take the masculine journey without at least one man by your side. Yes, there are times a man must face the battle alone, in the wee hours of the morn, and fight with all he's got. But don't make that a lifestyle of isolation.

We need men to whom we can bare our souls. But it isn't going to happen with a group of guys you don't trust, who really aren't willing to go to battle with you. It's a long-standing truth that there is never a more devoted group of men than those who have fought alongside one another, the men of your squadron, the guys in your foxhole. It will never be a large group, but you don't need a large group. You need a band of brothers willing to "shed their blood" with you.

Write out Ephesians 6:13–18 in the space below, underlining the specific elements that comprise the full armor of God.

Which part of the armor of God do you need to rely on more when battling the unholy trinity of the world, the flesh, and the devil?

It's never a good idea to go into battle alone. Do you have a band of brothers to walk with you through this life? If not, what are some steps for connecting with a few like-minded guys?

RECOMMENDED READING

Before your group gathers for the next session, read chapter 10, "A Beauty to Love," in *Wild at Heart*. This chapter will be the focus of session 5. Use the space below to write any key points or questions you want to bring to the next group meeting.

THE BEAUTY

Beauty is mysterious as well as terrible . . .
God and the Devil are fighting there, and the
battlefield is the heart of man.

FYODOR DOSTOYEVSKY

VIDEO TEACHING

Play the video segment for session 5. A summary of the key points is provided for your benefit as well as space to take additional notes.

Summary

In the story of the human race, God creates Adam and gives him a job as his partner running the world. But something is missing. In Genesis 2:20–23, we are told:

> *He gave names to all the livestock, all the birds of the sky, and all the wild animals. But still there was no helper just right for him.*
>
> *So the LORD God caused the man to fall into a deep sleep. While the man slept, the LORD God took out one of the man's ribs and closed up the opening. Then the LORD God made a woman from the rib, and he brought her to the man.*
>
> *"At last!" the man exclaimed* (NLT).

None of us have recovered from the surgery. We are haunted by Eve. She is wonderful. She is a mystery. The beauty of Eve is captivating. She feels like such a challenge to our masculinity. But learning to fight for the heart of a woman is absolutely core to what it means to be a man.

There is something so beautiful and inspiring about a woman. And when it comes to the woman we will fall in love with, the woman we want to marry and spend our life with, nothing can get the attention of a man like the beauty of a woman.

Beauty, love, sex—these things run deep in men, and they can feel like the biggest dilemma of our lives. If we look to a woman for affirmation or validation, it gets really messy. A real man goes to a woman to offer his strength, not to try and get his strength from her.

Now some words on Eve. She also bears the image of God. She also is wounded. She also has an enemy and a lot of agreements.

God made us warriors to fight for the hearts of the women in our lives. It takes courage to love. It takes resilience and a fierce heart. But this is what we are made for. To be the warrior on her behalf. To invite her into a great adventure.

A woman doesn't want to be the adventure. She wants to be invited up into one.

Notes

GROUP DISCUSSION

Take a few minutes to go through the following questions with your group.

1. What stood out to you about Alex's pursuit of his daughter's heart? Why?

2. When was your first crush? What did you like about her? What happened between you and her?

3. If you are married, how do you usually feel in the presence of your wife? Is it more thrilled, threatened, loving, strong, or like a boy? Explain.

4. "A woman's beauty is captivating, yet she also remains a mystery." Do you agree with that statement? Why or why not?

5. How much of your life have you spent looking to the woman for affirmation or validation? How has that gone for you?

6. Into what adventure can you invite your beauty? Rather than expect her to embrace your hobbies or interests, what is a shared adventure you can enjoy together?

RESPOND

Briefly review the summary for the session 5 teaching and any notes you took. In the space below, write down the most significant point you took away from this session.

CLOSING PRAYER

Wrap up your time together with prayer. Remember, prayer is simply talking to God. Here are a few ideas of what you could pray about based on the topics of this fifth session:

- Confess how you have often mishandled the beauty's heart.
- Name your desire to offer strength to a woman rather than take from her.
- Commit to seeking your validation from God rather than from women.
- Ask God how to pursue beauty, love, and sex from a healed, whole heart.
- Pray that God would show you how to fight for the heart of a woman.
- Seek God's counsel on how to invite your beauty into a shared adventure.

BETWEEN-SESSIONS PERSONAL STUDY

I n this section, you are invited to further explore the material in *Wild at Heart*. Each day's study in this section offers a short reading from chapter 10, "A Beauty to Love," of John's book, along with reflection questions designed to take you deeper into the themes of the study. Journal or just jot a few thoughts after each question. At the start of the next session, there will be a few minutes to share any insights . . . but remember that the primary goal of these questions is for your own personal growth and private reflection.

DAY ONE: EVE'S WOUND

Every woman can tell you about her wound; some came with violence, others came with neglect.

Just as every little boy is asking one question, every little girl is as well. But her question isn't so much about her strength. No, the deep cry of a little girl's heart is, *Do you see me? Am I worth choosing, worth fighting for? Am I lovely?* Every woman needs to know that she is exquisite and exotic and chosen. This is core to her identity, the way she bears the image of God. *Will you pursue me? Do you delight in me? Will you fight for me?* I am not saying every woman needs a man to be complete. *I am saying every woman wants to be loved, romanced, part of a shared adventure.*

And like every little boy, she has taken a wound as well. The wound strikes right at the core of her heart of beauty and leaves a devastating message with it: *No. You're not beautiful and no one will really fight for you.* Like your wound, hers almost always comes at the hand of her father.

A little girl looks to her father to know if she is lovely. The power he has to cripple or to bless is just as significant to her as it is to his son. If he's a violent man he may defile her verbally or sexually. What is a violated woman to think about her beauty? Am I lovely? The message is, *No . . . you are dirty. Anything attractive about you is dark and evil.* The assault continues as she grows up, through violent men and passive men. She may be stalked; she may be ignored. Either way, her heart is violated and the message is driven farther in: *you are not desired for your heart; you will not be protected; no one will fight for you.* The tower is built brick by brick, and when she's a grown woman it can be a fortress.

Like so many unloved young women, Stasi turned to boys to try to hear what she never heard from her father. Her high school boyfriend betrayed her on prom night, told her he had been using her, that he really loved someone else. The man she dated in college became verbally abusive. But when a woman never hears she's worth fighting for, she comes to believe that's the sort of treatment she deserves. It's a form of attention, in a twisted way; maybe it's better than nothing. Then we fell in love on that magical summer night. But Stasi married a frightened, driven man who had an affair with his work because he wouldn't risk engaging a woman he sensed he wasn't enough for. I wasn't mean; I wasn't evil. I was nice. And let me tell you, a hesitant man is the last thing in the world a woman needs. She needs a lover and a warrior, not a Really Nice Guy. Her worst fear was realized—I will never really be loved, never really be fought for. And so she hid some more.

Years into our marriage I found myself blindsided by it all. Where is the beauty I once saw? What happened to the woman I fell in love with? I didn't really expect an answer to my question; it was more a shout of rage than a desperate plea. But Jesus answered me anyway. *She's still in there; but she's captive. Are you willing to go in after her?* I realized that I had—like so many men—married for safety. I married a woman I thought would never challenge me as a man. Stasi adored me; what more did I need to do? I wanted to look like the knight, but I didn't want to bleed like one. I was deeply mistaken about the whole arrangement. I didn't know about the tower, or the dragon, or what my strength was for.

The number one problem between men and their women is that we men, when asked to truly fight for her . . . hesitate. We are still seeking to save ourselves; we have forgotten the deep pleasure of spilling our life for another.

What are the three questions of every young girl's heart?

How were those questions answered for the beauty in your life?

What relationship did the woman in your life have with her father when she was a girl? How can you fight for her heart in this area?

DAY TWO: OFFERING OUR STRENGTH

There are three things that are too amazing for me,
four that I do not understand:
the way of an eagle in the sky,
the way of a snake on a rock,
the way of a ship on the high seas,
and the way of a man with a young woman.

PROVERBS 30:18-19

Agur son of Jakeh is onto something here. There is something mythic in the way a man is with a woman. Our sexuality offers a parable of amazing depth when it comes to being masculine and feminine. The man comes to offer his strength and the woman invites the man into herself, an act that requires courage and vulnerability and selflessness for both of them. Notice first that if the man will not rise to the occasion, nothing will happen. He must move; his strength must swell before he can enter her. But neither will the love consummate unless the woman opens herself in stunning vulnerability. When both are living as they were meant to live, the man enters his woman and offers her his strength. He *spills himself there*, in her, for her; she draws him in, embraces and envelops him. When all is over he is spent; but ah, what a sweet death it is.

And that is how life is created.

The beauty of a woman arouses a man to play the man; the strength of a man, offered tenderly to his woman, allows her to be beautiful; it brings life to her and to many. This is far, far more than sex and orgasm. It is a reality that extends to every aspect of our lives. When a man withholds himself from his woman, he leaves her without the life only he can bring. This is never more true than with how a man offers—or does not offer—his words. Life and death are in the power of the tongue (see Proverbs 18:21). She is made for and craves words from him.

If the man refuses to offer himself, then his wife will remain empty and barren. A violent man destroys with his words; a silent man starves his wife. "She's wilting," a friend confessed to me about his new bride. "If she's wilting then you're withholding something," I said. Actually, it was several things—his words, his touch, but mostly his *delight*. There are so many other ways this plays out in life. A man who leaves his wife with the children and the bills to go and find another, easier life has denied them his strength. He has sacrificed them when he should have sacrificed his strength *for* them.

What makes Maximus or William Wallace so heroic is simply this: they are willing to die to set others free.

"They will be called oaks of righteousness" (Isaiah 61:3). There, under the shadow of a man's strength, a woman finds rest. The masculine journey takes a man away from the woman *so that he might return to her.* He goes to find his strength; he returns to offer it. He tears down the walls of the tower that has held her with his words and with his actions. He speaks to her heart's deepest question in a thousand ways. *Yes, you are lovely. Yes, there is one who will fight for you.* But because most men have not yet fought the battle, most women are still in the tower.

What do you think Proverbs 30:18–19 means regarding men and women?

A man is meant to freely offer and sacrifice his strength for those he loves. When have you had to come through for the beauty in your life in this way? What was her response?

"The tongue has the power of life and death" (Proverbs 18:21). A violent man destroys with his words. A silent man starves his wife. What impact do your words have on the beauty in your life?

DAY THREE: WHERE SO MANY MEN FALTER

Most men want the maiden without any sort of cost to themselves. They want all the joys of the beauty without any of the woes of the battle. This is the sinister nature of pornography—enjoying the woman at her expense. Pornography is what happens when a man insists on being energized by a woman; he *uses* her to get a feeling that he is a man. It is a false strength, as I've said, because it depends on an outside source rather than emanating from deep within his center. And it is the paragon of selfishness. He offers nothing and takes everything.

Women endure this abuse all the time. They are pursued, but not really; they are wanted, but only superficially. They learn to offer their bodies but never, ever their souls. Most men, you see, marry for safety; they choose a woman who will make them feel like a man but never really challenge them to be one. A young man whom I admire is wrestling between the woman he is dating and one he knew but could not capture years ago. Rachel, the woman he is currently dating, is asking a lot of him; truth be told, he feels in way over his head. Julie, the woman he did not pursue, seems more idyllic; in his imagination she would be the perfect mate. Life with Rachel is tumultuous; life with Julie seems calm and tranquil. "You want the Bahamas," I said. "Rachel is the North Atlantic. Which one requires a true man?" In a brilliant twist of plot, God turns our scheme for safety on us, requiring us to play the man.

Why don't men offer what they have to their women? Because we know down in our guts that it won't be enough. There is an emptiness to Eve after the Fall, and no matter how much you pour into her, she will never be filled. This is where so many men falter. Either they refuse to give what they can, or they keep pouring and pouring into her and all the while feel like a failure because she is still needing more. "There are three things that are never satisfied," warned Agur son of Jakeh, "four that never say, 'Enough!': the grave, the barren womb, land, which is never satisfied with water, and fire, which never says, 'Enough!'" (Proverbs 30:15–16).

The barrenness of Eve you can never hope to fill. She needs God more than she needs you, just as you need him more than you need her.

So what do you do? Offer what you have.

"I'm afraid it won't work," a client said to me when I suggested he move back toward his wife. "She's given up on me coming through for her," he confessed, "and that's good." "No, it's not," I said. "That's awful." He was headed to a family reunion back east, and I suggested he bring his wife with him, make it a vacation for the two of them. "You need to move toward her." "What if it doesn't work?" he asked.

So many men are asking the same question. Work for what? Validate you as a man? Resurrect her heart in a day?

Do you see now that you can't bring your question to Eve? No matter how good a man you are, you can never be enough. If she's the report card on your strength, then you'll ultimately get an F. But that's not why you love her—to get a good grade. You love her because that's what you are made to do; that's what a real man does.

Most men want the maiden without any cost to themselves. What has been the result when you've pursued a woman in this way? How did you feel about yourself afterward?

Pornography is enjoying the woman at her expense. It is the paragon of selfishness, where the man offers nothing and takes everything. Whether through pornography or in other ways, how have you taken from the beauty without offering anything in return?

How often do you offer your wife physical attention—holding hands, cuddling, a hug or kiss—without expecting it to lead to sex? How might things improve if you offered greater intimacy in these ways with nothing else demanded of her?

DAY FOUR: IT IS A BATTLE

Will you fight for her? That's the question Jesus asked me many years ago, right before our tenth anniversary, right at the time I was wondering what had happened to the woman I married. *You're on the fence, John,* he said. *Get in or get out.* I knew what he was saying—stop being a nice guy and act like a warrior. Play the man.

I brought flowers, took her to dinner, and began to move back toward her in my heart. But I knew there was more. That night, before we went to bed, I prayed for Stasi in a way I'd never prayed for her before. Out loud, before all the heavenly hosts, I stepped between her and the forces of darkness that had been coming against her. Honestly, I didn't really know what I was doing, only that I needed to take on the dragon. All hell broke loose. Everything we've learned about spiritual warfare began that night. And you know what happened? Stasi got free; the tower of her depression gave way as I began to truly fight for her.

And it's not just once, but again and again over time. That's where the myth really stumps us. Some men are willing to go in once, twice, even three times. But a warrior is in this for good. Oswald Chambers asked, "God spilt the life of his son that the world might be saved; are we prepared to spill out our lives?"[20]

A man I know named Daniel is in the midst of a very hard, very unpromising battle for his wife. It's been years now without much progress and without much hope. Sitting in a restaurant the other night, tears in his eyes, this is what he said to me: "I'm not going anywhere. This is my place in the battle. This is the hill that I will die on." He has reached a point that we all must come to, sooner or later, when it's no longer about winning or losing. His wife may respond and she may not. That's really no longer the issue. The question is simply this: *What kind of man do you want to be? Maximus? Wallace? Or Judah?* As a young pilot in the RAF wrote just before he went down in 1940, "The universe is so vast and so ageless that the life of one man can only be justified by the measure of his sacrifice."[21]

"Will you fight for her?" That is the question Jesus asked John. But it's also a question he asks of all men. How do you respond to that question?

105

Fighting for the beauty's heart is more than bringing flowers or taking her to dinner. It requires that you battle the spiritual warfare coming against her—not just once but regularly. How is the enemy coming against her currently? Are you willing to fight for her heart on this front?

In the fight for the beauty's heart, you must come to the point were it's no longer about winning or losing. She may respond . . . and she may not. That is no longer the issue. The question comes down to this: *What kind of man do you want to be?* How would you answer that question?

DAY FIVE: A VICTORY

Many years ago, eighteen years into our marriage, Stasi and I attended a friend's wedding. It was the best nuptials either of us had ever been to; a wonderful, romantic, holy affair. The groom was young and strong and valiant; the bride was seductively beautiful. Which is what made it so excruciating for me. Oh, to start over again, to do it all over the right way, marry as a young man knowing what I know now. I could have loved Stasi so much better; she could have loved me so much better as well.

We've learned every lesson the hard way over our almost forty years. Any wisdom contained in these pages was paid for, dearly. On top of that, Stasi and I were in a difficult place over that weekend. Every man has his struggles; every marriage has its rough spots; every ministry has personal conflicts. Those issues are like a campfire that the enemy throws gasoline all over and turns into a bonfire. Satan saw his opportunity and turned it into a bonfire *without even one word between us*. By the time we got to the reception, I didn't want to dance with her. I didn't even want to be in the same room. All the hurt and disappointment of the years—hers and mine—seemed to be the only thing that was ever true about our marriage.

It wasn't until later that I heard Stasi's side of the script, but here is how the two fit together. Stasi: *He's disappointed in me. No wonder why. Look at all these beautiful women. I feel fat and ugly.* Me: *I'm so tired of battling for our marriage. How I wish we could start over. It wouldn't be that hard, you know. There are other options. Look at all these beautiful women.* On and on it came, like a wave overwhelming the shore. Sitting at the table with a group of our friends, I felt I was going to suffocate; I had to get out of there, get some fresh air.

Truth be told, when I left the reception I had no intention of going back. Either I'd wind up in a bar somewhere or back in our room watching TV. Thankfully, I found a small library off to the side of the reception hall; alone in that sanctuary I wrestled with all I was feeling for what seemed like an hour. (It was probably twenty minutes.) I grabbed a book but could not read; I tried to pray but did not want to. Finally, some words began to arise from my heart:

> *Jesus, come and rescue me. I know what's going on; I know this
> is assault. But right now it all feels so true. Jesus, deliver me. Get
> me out from under this waterfall. Speak to me; rescue my heart
> before I do something stupid. Deliver me, Lord.*

Slowly, almost imperceptibly, the wave began to lift. My
thoughts and emotions quieted down to a more normal size.
Clarity was returning. The campfire was just a campfire
again. *Jesus, you know the pain and disappointment in my heart.
What would you have me do?* (The bar was no longer an option,
but I was still planning to just go straight to my room for the
rest of the night.) *I want you to go back in there and ask your wife
to dance.* I knew he was right; I knew that somewhere down
deep inside that's what my true heart would want to do. But
the desire still seemed so far away. I lingered for five more
minutes, hoping he had another option for me. He remained
silent, but the assault was over and the bonfire was only
embers. Once more I knew the man I wanted to be.

I went back to the reception and asked Stasi to dance;
for the next two hours we had one of the best evenings we've
had in a long time. We nearly lost to the evil one; instead, it
will go down as a memory we'll share with our friends for a
long, long time.

What part of John and Stasi's story at the wedding reception
could you relate to the most? Why?

The turning point in the story came when John began to pray. What did he ask Jesus to do for him? What did John name was really going on—in spite of what felt so true?

What is one word you will say and one action you will do this week to win the heart of your beauty?

RECOMMENDED READING

Before your group gathers for the next session, read chapter 11, "An Adventure to Live," in *Wild at Heart.* This chapter will be the focus of session 6. Use the space below to write any key points or questions you want to bring to the next group meeting.

THE ADVENTURE

The place where God calls you is the place where your deep gladness and the world's deep hunger meet.

FREDERICK BUECHNER

VIDEO TEACHING

Play the video segment for session 6. A summary of the key points is provided for your benefit as well as space to take additional notes.

Summary

Throughout our time together, we've been following the story of Adam through the opening pages of Genesis.

Have you ever considered that Adam was given the most incredible birthday present ever? God gave him this wild, beautiful world. Rivers. Jungle. Mountains. Ocean. All his to discover and explore.

No song has been written. No mountain has been climbed. No one has figured out geometry or physics or how to make coffee. The whole wild world lies before him. To rule. To subdue. To have a fierce mastery over.

As men, we are wired for adventure. These adventures come in three different forms.

First, there is *casual* adventure. We love to fish, ski, or travel. These are the daily or weekly things that feed and nourish the masculine soul.

Next is *crucial* adventure. This goes deeper—and is tied to our calling, our career, or our mission in life. We may decide to go to grad school, start a company, or join the military. Every man needs a mission to his life. We need to be careful here, as our mission may not be our career. (Paul made tents for a living.)

Finally, there is *critical* adventure. This is the deepest of all. It involves intimate partnership with God. Look at the story of Joseph, David, Paul, and the disciples.

The amount of risk with which you are willing to live is a direct correlation to what you believe about God. You cannot master enough principles to figure out every dynamic situation. Nor do you need to. You have something far better—friendship with Jesus.

It's never too late to pursue adventure. I've seen men sixty-five, seventy-five, and eighty-five years old get their hearts back and begin to live as they always wanted to live. Living as the sons of God. Living as really good men.

God has wired you for adventure in very specific ways. Now it's time to follow him into the adventures that he has for you.

Notes

GROUP DISCUSSION

Take a few minutes to go through the following questions with your group.

1. How did Morgan's story stir your desire for adventure?

2. A man won't be happy until he has adventure in his work, his love, and his spiritual life. Where are you currently finding adventure in each of these areas?

3. What casual adventure are you pursuing? What do you most enjoy about it?

4. What is your current crucial adventure? Why is this important to you?

5. How would you describe your critical adventure? Why do you feel that God has put this mission on your heart?

6. What adventure have you written off as too late, too big, or too impossible to pursue? How might it change things to realize that God often invites us into adventures we can't do alone—ones that are only possible with him?

RESPOND

Briefly review the summary for the session 6 teaching and any notes you took. In the space below, write down the most significant point you took away from this session.

CLOSING PRAYER

Wrap up your time together with prayer. Remember, prayer is simply talking to God. Here are a few ideas of what you could pray about based on the topics of this final session:

- Acknowledge how your desire for control gets in the way of adventure.
- Pray for God to draw your heart to true adventure.
- Ask God to help you overcome your fear of risk.
- Name the adventures you desire in your work, love, and spiritual life.
- Express your appreciation that there are no formulas with God.
- Declare your desire for the kind of adventures that can only be realized with God.

BETWEEN-SESSIONS PERSONAL STUDY

I n this section, you are invited to further explore the material in *Wild at Heart*. Each day's study in this section offers a short reading from chapter 11, "An Adventure to Love," of John's book, along with reflection questions designed to take you deeper into the themes of the study. In this final time of personal study, journal or just jot a few thoughts after each question for your growth and private reflection.

DAY ONE: ASKING THE RIGHT QUESTION

Life is not a problem to be solved; it is an adventure to be lived. That's the nature of it, and has been since the beginning when God set the dangerous stage for this high-stakes drama and called the whole wild enterprise *good*. He rigged the world in such a way that it only works when we embrace *risk* as the theme of our lives, which is to say, only when we live by faith. A man just won't be happy until he's got adventure in his work, in his love, and in his spiritual life.

Several years ago, I was thumbing through the introduction of a book when I ran across a sentence that changed my life. God is intimately personal with us and he speaks in ways that are peculiar to our own quirky hearts—not just through the Bible, but through the whole of creation. To Stasi he speaks through movies. To my friend Craig, he speaks through rock and roll (he called me the other day after listening to "Running Through the Jungle" to say he was fired up to go study the Bible). God's word to me comes in many ways—through sunsets and friends and films and music and wilderness and books.

But he's got an especially humorous thing going with me and books. I'll be browsing through a secondhand bookshop when out of a thousand volumes one will say, "Pick me up"—just like Augustine in his *Confessions*. *Tolle legge*—take up and read. Like a master fly fisherman, God cast his fly to this cruising trout. In the introduction to the book that I rose to this day, the author, Gil Bailie, shares a piece of advice given to him some years back by a spiritual mentor, Howard Thurman:

> *Don't ask yourself what the world needs. Ask yourself what makes you come alive, and go do that, because what the world needs is people who have come alive.*[22]

I was struck dumb. It could have been Balaam's donkey, for all I was concerned. Suddenly my life up till that point made sense in a sickening sort of way; I realized I was living a script written for me by someone else. All my life I had been asking the world to tell me what to do with myself. This is different from seeking counsel or advice; what I wanted was freedom from responsibility and especially freedom from risk. I wanted someone else to tell me who to be.

Thank God it didn't work. The scripts they handed me I simply could not bring myself to play for very long. Like Saul's armor, they never fit. Can a world of posers tell you to do anything but pose yourself? As Frederick Buechner said, we are in constant danger of being not actors in the drama of our lives but reactors, "to go where the world takes us, to drift with whatever current happens to be running the strongest."[23] Reading the counsel Thurman gave to Bailie, I knew it was God speaking to me. It was an invitation to come out of Ur.

I set the volume down without turning another page and walked out of that bookstore to find a life worth living.

Life is not a problem to be solved; it is an adventure to be lived. What does that statement stir in your heart? Why?

Howard Thurman said, "Don't ask yourself what the world needs. Ask yourself what makes you come alive, and go do that, because what the world needs is people who have come alive." What makes *you* come alive?

John shared how he realized he was living a script written for him by someone else. Can you relate to that feeling? If so, how is God inviting you into the adventure you were born to live?

DAY TWO: WHAT ARE YOU WAITING FOR?

Where would we be today if Abraham had carefully weighed the pros and cons of God's invitation and decided that he'd rather hang on to his medical benefits, three weeks paid vacation, and retirement plan in Ur? What would have happened if Moses had listened to his mother's advice to "never play with matches" and lived a careful, cautious life steering clear of all burning bushes? You wouldn't have the gospel if Paul had concluded that the life of a Pharisee, while not everything a man dreams for, was at least predictable and certainly more stable than following a voice he heard on the Damascus road. After all, people hear voices all the time and who really knows whether it's God or just one's imagination. Where would we be if Jesus was not fierce and wild and romantic to the core? Come to think of it, we wouldn't *be* at all if God hadn't taken that enormous risk of creating us in the first place.

Most men spend the energy of their lives trying to eliminate risk, or squeezing it down to a more manageable size. Their children hear "no" far more than they hear "yes"; their employees feel chained up and their wives are equally bound. If it works, if a man succeeds in securing his life against all risk, he'll wind up in a cocoon of self-protection and wonder all the while why he's suffocating. If it doesn't work, he curses God and redoubles his efforts and his blood pressure. When you look at the structure of the false self that men tend to create, it always revolves around two themes: seizing upon some sort of competence and rejecting anything that cannot be controlled. As David Whyte said, "The price of our vitality is the sum of all our fears."[24]

For murdering his brother, God sentenced Cain to the life of a restless wanderer; five verses later Cain is building a city (see Genesis 4:12, 17). That sort of commitment—the refusal to trust God and the reach for control—runs deep in every man. Whyte talks about the difference between the false self's desire "to have power *over* experience, to control all events and consequences, and the soul's wish to have power *through* experience, *no matter what that may be*."[25] You literally sacrifice your soul and your true power when you insist on controlling things, like the guy Jesus talked about who thought he had finally pulled it all off, built himself some really nice barns, and died the same night. "What will it profit a man if he gains the whole world, and loses his own soul?" (Mark 8:36 NKJV).

You can lose your soul, by the way, long before you die.

John notes that God took an enormous risk in creating us in the first place. How would you describe that risk?

Most men spend their energy in life trying to eliminate risk or squeeze it down to a more manageable size. Would you say this describes you? Why or why not?

Why do you think the refusal to trust God and the reach for control runs deep in every man?

DAY THREE: THE RECOVERY OF DREAMS

Something in us remembers, however faintly, that when God set man on the earth, he gave us an incredible mission—a charter to explore, build, conquer, and care for all creation. It was a blank page waiting to be written; a clean canvas waiting to be painted. Well, sir, God never revoked that charter. It's still there, waiting for a man to seize it.

If you had permission to do what you really want to do, what would you do? Don't ask *how*; that will cut your desire off at the knees. *How* is never the right question; *how* is a faithless question. It means "unless I can see my way clearly I won't believe it, won't venture forth." When the angel told Zechariah that his ancient wife would bear him a son named John, Zechariah asked how and was struck dumb for it.

How is God's department. He is asking you *what*. What is written in your heart? What makes you come alive? If you could do what you've always wanted to do, what would it be? You see, a man's calling is written on his true heart, and he discovers it when he enters the frontier of his deep desires. To paraphrase Howard Thurman's advice to Gil Bailie, don't ask yourself what the world needs; ask yourself what makes you come alive, because what the world needs are *men* who have come alive.

The invitation in the bookshop, I must note, was given to me some years into my Christian life when the transformation of my character was at a point that I could hear it without running off and doing something stupid. I've met men who've used advice like it as permission to leave their wife and run off with their secretary. They are *deceived* about what it is they are made for. There is a design God has woven into the fabric of this world, and if we violate it we cannot hope to find life.

> *What does the LORD your God ask of you but to fear the LORD your God, to walk in obedience to him, to love him, to serve the LORD your God with all your heart and with all your soul, and to observe the LORD's commands and decrees that I am giving you today for your own good?*
>
> DEUTERONOMY 10:12-13

Because our hearts have strayed so far from home, he's given us the Law as a sort of handrail to help us back from the precipice. But the goal of Christian discipleship is the transformed heart; we move from a boy who needs the Law to the man who is able to live by the Spirit of the Law. "My counsel is this: Live freely, animated and motivated by God's Spirit. Then you won't feed the compulsions of selfishness.... Legalism is helpless in bringing this about; it only gets in the way" (Galatians 5:16, 23 MSG).

A man's life becomes an adventure, the whole thing takes on a transcendent purpose when he releases control in exchange for the recovery of the dreams in his heart.

If you could do what you've always wanted to do, what would it be? How would pursuing that adventure make you come alive?

Why is *how* never the right question when considering a longing that God has put in your heart?

The goal of Christian discipleship is the transformed heart. How does Deuteronomy 10:12–13 and Galatians 5:16, 23 reflect the progression from a boy who needs the Law to the man who is able to live by the Spirit of the Law? Where are you in this journey?

DAY FOUR: INTO THE UNKNOWN

"The spiritual world . . . cannot be made suburban," said Howard Macey. "It is always frontier and we who live in it must accept and even rejoice that it remains untamed."[26] The greatest obstacle to realizing our dreams is the false self's hatred of mystery. That's a problem, you see, because *mystery is essential to adventure*. More than that, mystery is the heart of the universe and the God who made it. The most important aspects of any man's world—his relationship with his God and with the people in his life, his calling, the spiritual battles he'll face—every one of them is fraught with mystery. But that is not a bad thing; it is a joyful, rich part of reality and essential to our soul's thirst for adventure. As Oswald Chambers said:

> *Naturally, we are inclined to be so mathematical and calculating that we look upon uncertainty as a bad thing . . . Certainty is the mark of the common-sense life; gracious uncertainty is the mark of the spiritual life. To be certain of God means that we are uncertain in all our ways, we do not know what a day may bring forth. This is generally said with a sigh of sadness; it should rather be an expression of breathless expectation.*[27]

There are no formulas with God. Period. So there are no formulas for the man who follows him.

God is a Person, not a doctrine. He operates not like a system—not even a theological system—but with all the originality of a truly free and alive person. "The realm of God is dangerous," said Archbishop Anthony Bloom. "You must enter into it and not just seek information about it."[28]

The Modern Era hates mystery; we desperately want a means of controlling our own lives, and we seem to have found the ultimate Tower of Babel in the scientific method. Don't get me wrong—science has given us many wonderful advances in sanitation, medicine, transportation. But we've tried to use those methods to tame the wildness of the spiritual frontier. We take the latest marketing methods, the newest business management fad, and we apply it to ministry. The problem with modern Christianity's obsession with principles is that it removes any real conversation with God. Find the principle, apply the principle—what do you need God for? So Oswald Chambers warned us, "Never make a principle out of your experience; let God be as original with other people as he is with you."[29]

Originality and creativity are essential to personhood and to masculine strength. The adventure begins and our *real* strength is released when we no longer rely on formulas. God is an immensely creative Person, and he wants his sons to live that way too.

Why do you think mystery is such an essential part of the adventures that God has for us?

Does the statement that "there are no formulas with God" comfort you or frustrate you? Why?

Originality and creativity are essential to having a masculine strength. Where do you see these attributes in God? Where do you see them in your life?

DAY FIVE: FROM FORMULA TO RELATIONSHIP

The only way to live in this adventure—with all its danger and unpredictability and immensely high stakes—is in an ongoing, intimate relationship with God. The control we so desperately crave is an illusion. Far better to give it up in exchange for God's offer of companionship, set aside stale formulas so that we might enter into an informal friendship.

Abraham knew this; Moses did as well. Read through the first several chapters of Exodus—it's filled with a give-and-take between Moses and God. "Then the Lord said to Moses," (Exodus 6:1); "but Moses said to the Lord" (verse 12). The two act like they know each other, like they really are intimate allies. David—a man after God's own heart—also walked and warred and loved his way through life in a conversational intimacy with God:

> When the Philistines heard that David had been anointed king over Israel, they went up in full force to search for him, but David heard about it and went down to the stronghold. Now the Philistines had come and spread out in the Valley of Rephaim; so David inquired of the LORD, "Shall I go and attack the Philistines? Will you hand them over to me?"
>
> The LORD answered him, "Go, for I will surely hand the Philistines over to you."
>
> So David went to Baal Perazim, and there he defeated them . . . Once more the Philistines came up and spread out in the Valley of Rephaim; so David inquired of the LORD, and he answered, "Do not go straight up, but circle around behind them and attack them in front of the balsam trees. As soon as you hear the sound of marching in the tops of the balsam trees, move quickly, because that will mean the LORD has gone out in front of you to strike the Philistine army." So David did as the LORD commanded him, and he struck down the Philistines all the way from Gibeon to Gezer.
>
> 2 SAMUEL 5:17-20, 22-25 NIV 84

Here again, there is no rigid formula for David; it changes as he goes, relying on the counsel of God. This is the way every comrade and close companion of God lives. Jesus said, "I no longer call you servants, because a servant does not know his master's business. Instead, I have called you friends, for everything that I learned from my father I have made known to you" (John 15:15). God calls you his friend. He wants to talk to you—personally, frequently.

As Dallas Willard wrote, "The ideal for hearing from God is . . . a conversational relationship with God: the sort of relationship suited to friends who are mature personalities in a shared enterprise."[30] Our whole journey into authentic masculinity centers around those cool-of-the-day talks with God. Simple questions change hassles to adventures; the events of our lives become opportunities for initiation. "What are you teaching me here, God? What are you asking me to do . . . or to let go of? What in my heart are you speaking to?"

Men desperately crave control. Why does it often feel more appealing to pursue control than companionship with God?

What does the story of David and the Philistines reveal about the ways of God? How might this understanding help you approach a challenging situation differently?

Our journey into authentic masculinity centers around conversations with God. Simple questions change hassles to adventures; the events of our lives become opportunities for initiation. What current or coming adventure do you need to discuss with God? How might it change if you saw it as an invitation into initiation?

RECOMMENDED READING

Well done! You've completed the study, yet there is much more in the book (including chapters 5, 6, and 12) than we could cover in six sessions. We hope that you will take the time to read *Wild at Heart* cover to cover. It will change your world! From there, you can continue the journey at www.wildatheart.org, where you'll find weekly podcasts, a wealth of free audio and video resources, event updates, and more.

LEADER'S GUIDE

Thank you for your willingness to lead your group through *Wild at Heart: Discovering the Secret of a Man's Soul*. The rewards of leading are different from the rewards of participating, and we hope you find your own walk with Jesus deepened by this experience. This leader's guide will give you some tips on how to prepare for your time together and facilitate a meaningful experience for your group members.

WHAT DOES IT TAKE TO LEAD THIS STUDY?

Get together and watch God show up. Seriously, that's the basics of how a small group works. Gather several people together who have a hunger for God, want to learn how to get their lives back, and are willing to be open and honest with God and themselves. The Lord will honor this every time and show up in the group. You don't have to be a pastor, priest, theologian, or counselor to lead a group through this study. Just invite people over, watch the video, and talk about it. All you need is a willing heart, a little courage, and God will do the rest. Really.

HOW THIS STUDY WORKS

As the group leader, you will want to make sure everyone in your group has a copy of this study guide. (The group members will also want to have a copy of the *Wild at Heart* book if they are doing the recommended readings for each session.) It works best if you can get the guides (and books) to your group *before* the first meeting. That way, everyone can read the material in the book ahead of time and be prepared to watch the first video session together.

This series is presented in six video sessions, with each session being approximately fifteen to twenty minutes in length. Each week, you will meet together to watch the video and discuss the session. This series can also be used in classroom settings, such as Sunday school classes, though you may need to modify the discussion time depending on the size of the class. You could even use the video as sessions for a special prayer retreat.

Basically, each week you will: (1) watch the video sessions, (2) talk about them, and (3) reflect on what you have learned by completing the between-sessions activities. That's it!

A FEW TIPS FOR LEADING A GROUP

The setting really matters. If you can choose to meet in a living room over a conference room in a church, do it. Pick an environment that's conducive to people relaxing and getting real. Remember the enemy likes to distract us when it comes to seeking God, so do what you can to remove these obstacles from your group (silence cell phones, limit background noise, no texting). Set the chairs or couches in a circle to prevent having a "classroom" feel.

Have some refreshments! Coffee and water will do; cookies and snacks are even better. People tend to be nervous when they join a new group, so if you can give them something to hold onto (like a warm mug of coffee), they will relax a lot more. It's human nature.

Good equipment is important. Meet where you can watch the video sessions on a screen big enough for everyone to see and enjoy. Get or borrow the best gear you can. Also, be sure to test your media equipment ahead of time to make sure everything is in working condition. This way, if something isn't working, you can fix it or make other arrangements before the meeting begins. (You'll be amazed at how the enemy will try to mess things up for you!)

Be honest. Remember that your honesty will set the tone for your time together. Be willing to answer questions personally, as this will set the pace for the length of your group members' responses and will make others more comfortable in sharing.

Stick to the schedule. Strive to begin and end your meetings at the same time each week. The people in your group are busy, and if they can trust you to be a good steward of their time, they will be more willing to come back each week. Of course, you want to be open to the work God is doing, and at times you may want to *linger* in prayer or discussion. Remember the clock serves *you;* your group doesn't serve the clock. But work to respect the group's time, especially when it comes to limiting the discussion times.

Don't be afraid of silence or emotion. Welcome awkward moments. The material presented during this study will challenge the group members to reconsider some of their beliefs and compel them to make the necessary changes in their lives. Don't be afraid to ease into the material with the group.

Don't dominate the conversation. Even though you are the leader, you are also a member of this small group. So don't steamroll over others in an attempt to lead—and don't let anyone else in the group do so either.

Prepare for your meeting. Watch the video for the meeting ahead of time. Although it may feel a bit like cheating because you'll know what's coming, you will be better prepared for what the session might stir in the hearts of your group members. Also be sure to review the material in this guide and spend some time in prayer. In fact, the *most important* thing you can do is simply pray ahead of time each week:

> *Lord Jesus, come and rule this time. Let your Spirit fill this place. Bring your kingdom here. Take us right to the things we really need to talk about and rescue us from every distraction. Show us the heart of the Father. Meet each person here. Give us your grace and love for one another. In your name I pray.*

Make sure your group members are prepared. Before the first meeting, secure enough copies of the study guide for each member. Have these ready and on hand for the first meeting, or make sure the participants have purchased them. Send out a reminder email or a text a couple of days before the meeting to make sure folks don't forget about it.

AS YOU GATHER

You will find the following counsel to be especially helpful when you meet for the first time as a group. I offer these comments in the spirit of "here is what I would do if I were leading a group through this study."

First, as the group gathers, start your time with introductions if people don't know each other. Begin with yourself and share your name, how long you've been a follower of Christ, if you have a spouse and/or children, and what you want to learn most from this study. Going first will put the group more at ease.

After the introductions, jump right into watching the video teaching, as this will help get things started on a strong note. In the following weeks, you may want to start by allowing folks to catch up a little with some "how are you?" kind of banter. Too much of this burns up your meeting time, but you have to allow some room for it because it helps build relationships among the group members.

Note that each group will have its own personality and dynamics. Typically, people will hold back the first week or two until they feel the group is "safe." Then they will begin to share. Again, don't let it throw you if your group seems a bit awkward at first. Of course, some people *never* want to talk, so you'll need to coax them out as time goes on. But let it go the first week.

INSIGHT FOR DISCUSSION

If the group members are in any way open to talking about their lives as it relates to this material, you will likely *not* have enough time for every question suggested in this study guide. That's okay! Pick the questions ahead of time that you know you definitely want to cover, just in case you end up only having time to discuss a few of them.

You set the tone for the group. Your honesty and vulnerability during discussion times will tell them what they can share. How *long* you talk will give them an example of how long they should respond. So give some thought to what stories or insights from your own work in the study guide you want to highlight.

WARNING: The greatest temptation for most small group leaders is to add to the video teaching with a little "teaching session" of their own. This is unhelpful for three reasons:

1. The discussion time will be the richest time during your meeting. The video sessions have been intentionally kept short so you can have plenty of time for discussion. If you add to the teaching, you sacrifice this precious time.

2. You don't want your group members *teaching, lecturing,* or *correcting* one another. The group members are all at a different place in their spiritual journey. If you set a tone by teaching, the group will feel like they have the freedom to teach one another. That can be disastrous for group dynamics.

3. The participants will be watching the video teachings during your group time and exploring the topics in more detail by completing the between-sessions activities. They don't need more content! What they want is a chance to talk and process their own lives in light of all they have taken in.

A STRONG CLOSE

Some of the best learning times will take place after the group time as God brings new insights to the participants during the week. Encourage group members to write down any questions they have as they work through the between-sessions exercises. Make sure they know you are available for them as they explore the material. Finally, make sure you close your time by praying together—either by following the suggested prompts or coming up with your own closing prayers. Ask two or three people to pray, inviting God to fill your group and lead each person during this study.

Thanks again for taking the time to lead your group. May God reward your efforts to help men recover their masculine hearts!

ENDNOTES

1. D. H. Lawrence, "Healing," in *The Rag and Bone Shop of the Heart: A Poetry Anthology*, ed. Robert Bly, James Hillman, and Michael Meade (New York: HarperCollins, 1992), 113.
2. Robert Bly, *Iron John: A Book About Men, 25th Anniversary Edition* (Philadelphia, PA: Da Capo Press, 2015), 64, 6.
3. Walter Brueggemann, *A Commentary on Jeremiah: Exile and Homecoming* (Grand Rapids, MI: Wm. B. Eerdmans Publishing Co., 1998), commentary on Jeremiah 14:17–22, 138.
4. Bly, *Iron John: A Book About Men, 25th Anniversary Edition*, 64, 6.
5. Garrison Keillor, *The Book of Guys* (New York: Penguin Books, 1993), 17–18.
6. I'm indebted to Crabb, Hudson, and Andrews for pointing this out in *The Silence of Adam*.
7. Leanne Payne, *Crisis in Masculinity* (Grand Rapids, MI: Hamewith Books [1985], 2006), 12.
8. Agnes Sanford, *The Healing Gifts of the Spirit* (New York: HarperCollins, 1984), 126–127.
9. C.S. Lewis, *Mere Christianity* (New York: HarperCollins, 2015), 227.
10. George MacDonald, *Diary of an Old Soul* (Eastford, CT: Martino Publishing [1880], 2015), 26.
11. Saint Augustine, *Confessions*, ed. R. S. Pine-Coffin (London: Penguin Books, 1961), 202.
12. George MacDonald, *Unspoken Sermons Series I, II, and III* (New York: Start Publishing [1867] 2012), 148.
13. Robert Bly, *Iron John: A Book About Men, 25th Anniversary Edition* (Philadelphia, PA: Da Capo Press, 2015), 25.
14. Neil T. Anderson, *The Bondage Breaker* (Eugene, OR: Harvest House Publishers [1990] 2006), 224–225.
15. Anderson, *The Bondage Breaker*, 224–225.
16. Winston Churchill, *The Second World War Volume I: The Gathering Storm* (New York: Houghton Mifflin Company [1948] 1986), 601.

17. John Owen, *Overcoming Sin and Temptation*, ed. Kelly M. Kapic and Justin Taylor (Wheaton, IL: Crossway, 2015), 171.
18. MacDonald, *Unspoken Sermons Series I, II, and III*, 120.
19. William Gurnall, *The Christian in Complete Armour: Daily Readings in Spiritual Warfare*, ed. James S. Bell Jr. (Chicago: Moody Press, 1994), 11.
20. Oswald Chambers, *My Utmost for His Highest: Classic Edition* (Grand Rapids, MI: Discovery House, (1927) 2017), 9/2.
21. Vivian William Noall Rosewarne, "An Airman's Letter to His Mother, April 1940," in "An Airman to His Mother: The Fight with Evil," *The Times*, June 18, 1940.
22. Howard Thurman as quoted in: Gil Bailie, *Violence Unveiled: Humanity at the Crossroads* (New York: Crossroad, 1995), xv.
23. Frederick Buechner, *The Longing for Home: Recollections and Reflections* (New York: HarperCollins, 1996), 109.
24. David Whyte, *The Heart Aroused: Poetry and the Preservation of the Soul in Corporate America* (New York: Doubleday [1994] 2007), 29.
25. Whyte, 17.
26. Howard R. Macy, *Rhythms of the Inner Life: Yearning for Closeness with God* (Colorado Springs, CO: Chariot Victor Publishing, 1999), 130.
27. Chambers, *My Utmost for His Highest: Classic Edition*, 4/29.
28. Anthony Bloom, *Beginning to Pray* (New York: Paulist Press, 1970), 15.
29. Chambers, *My Utmost for His Highest*, 6/13.
30. Dallas Willard, *Hearing God: Developing a Conversational Relationship with God* (Downers Grove, IL: InterVarsity Press, 2012), 35.

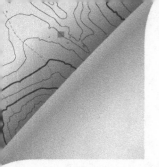

Finishing this study is only the beginning.

Continue your journey at
WildAtHeart.org

Weekly Podcasts

Video & Audio Resources

Prayers We Pray

Live Events

 Download the **Wild at Heart App**.

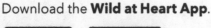

Wild At Heart in your world.

BASIC

Join John Eldredge and his team for this exclusive Wild At Heart Boot Camp video event. Find a BASIC near you or start your own at:

wildatheart.org/basic

A Journey into
What It Means to Be a Man

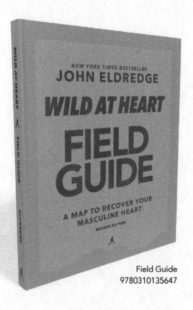

Field Guide
9780310135647

Sometime between boyhood and the struggles of yesterday, most men lose heart. All their passions, dreams, and desires get buried under deadlines, pressures, and disappointments.

The Wild at Heart Field Guide is geared to help you counter this trend, enter into wholeheartedness, and uncover the true secret of the masculine soul. It takes you from reading about the wild heart to living from it.

Packed with information and insights, this guide invites you onto "the road less traveled." It follows the *Wild at Heart* book but adds powerful questions, creative exercises, and space for you to record personal notes along the way. If you're ready to come alive again and find your great battle, adventure, and beauty . . . here is the map for recovering your masculine heart.

Available now at your favorite bookstore,
or streaming video on StudyGateway.com.

THOMAS NELSON
Since 1798